Subjects of Crisis

Subjects of Crisis

Race and Gender as Disease in Latin America

Benigno Trigo

Wesleyan University Press

Published by University Press of New England

Hanover and London

Wesleyan University Press

Published by University Press of New England, Hanover, NH 03755

Printed in the United States of America

5 4 3 2 1

CIP data appear at the end of the book

I am grateful to my family, and in particular to Mami, my first reader ever, who encouraged me to continue to write. Most of all, I wish to thank mi Kelly querida. Without whose love, dedication, conversation, encouragement, and inspiration I would never have written this book. Juntos en la escritura.

Contents

Illustrations

Acknowledgments

I am convinced that I cannot not write without friends. I need their motivation, inspiration, and support. I need their suggestions, their attention, their generosity. I need their words and affection. I would like to take this opportunity to express my gratitude to Ben Apt, Aida Beaupied, Hugo Biagini, Purnima Bose, Antonio Benítez Rojo, Román de la Campa, Jorge Castillo, Rex Clark, Harvey Cormier, Laura Dassow Walls, Penelope Deutscher, Fernando Feliú, Lee Fontanella, Anibal González, Vance Holloway, Sonia Labrador-Rodríguez, Naomi Lindstrom, Misha, Sylvia Molloy, Gabriela Nouzeilles, John Ochoa, Kelly Oliver, Julio Ramos, Katheryn Ríos, Nicolas Shumway, Linda Simon, Elzbieta Sklodowska, Dan Smulian, Ilan Stavans, Doris Sommer, Melbourne Tapper, Chris Thomas, and Fernando Unzueta. All of them, at one point or another, helped me to write this book.

I would also like to thank Suzanna Tamminen, my editor at Wesleyan University Press, as well as Matthew Byrnie and the staff of the University Press of New England.

A long project like this book also benefits from the insightful commentary offered by students in my classes. I am eternally grateful to them. I am indebted to the generosity of graduate students at the University of Texas, particularly to my friends, Guillermo Irizarry, Nancy La Greca, Patricia Lebo, and María Zalduondo.

I am also grateful for the support of all my friends and colleagues at the University of Texas: Matthew Bailey, Christine Barber-Nicolopulos, Kit Belgum, Bob Brody, José Cerna-Bazán, Catherine Echols, Cristina Ferreira-Pinto, Enrique Fierro, Ricardo González, Michael Harney, Aline Helg, Lily Litvak, Lisa Moore, Donnete Moss, Olga Negrón, Jaime Nicolopulos, Debbie Nelson, Norman Prentice, Cory Reed, César Salgado, Madeline Sutherland-Meier, Christine Williams, Jacquie Wooley, and Stan Zimic.

I would also like to thank the members of the Disease, Culture, and Identity Working Group at the University of Texas (Leslie Dean Jones, Sonia Arbona, Mel Tapper, and Janna Weiss) for their critical remarks, as well as for their timely encouragement.

Economic support for this research was provided by the Institute of Latin American Studies at the University of Texas at Austin from funds granted to the Institute by the Andrew W. Mellon Foundation, and by the University of Texas at Austin Summer Research Award. Portions of this book appeared in *Journal of Latin American Cultural Studies*, and in *Comparative Studies in Society and History*: a version of chapter 4 appeared in *Journal of Latin American Cultural Studies* 6.1 (1997): 7–20; a version of chapter 3 appeared in *Comparative Studies in Society and History* 41:1 (January 1999). I am grateful to the editors for permission to reprint them in revised form.

Subjects of Crisis

Introduction

The race question is a very serious problem in American history: it explains the progress of some nations, the decadence of others; it is the key to the incurable malady which is lacerating America.
——Francisco García Calderón, *Les démocraties latines de l'Amérique*

We must agree, frankly, vigorously, and directly, that we are sick; or rather, that we have been born sick and that our total collapse may be certain.
——Alcides Arguedas, *Pueblo enfermo*

A majority of Latin American intellectuals of the turn of the nineteenth century represented Latin America as a region in crisis. Martin Stabb has convincingly shown that writers from South and Central America saw that region as a "sick continent."[1] The titles of such works as the political pamphlet *The Diseased Continent* (1899) by the Venezuelan César Zumeta, and the sociological and anthropological treatise *Diseased People* (1909) by the Bolivian Alcides Arguedas, bear him out. The title of the literary trilogy *Chronicle of a Diseased People* (1894–1925) by the Puerto Rican doctor Manuel Zeno Gandía further expands Stabb's insight to the Caribbean region, and to the first quarter of the twentieth century.

Disease in these titles is a metaphor for a general state of crisis that these writers found not only in their respective regions, but also throughout Latin America. Like many of their contemporaries, they believed that Latin America (its peoples, geographies, societies, economies, and cultures), was at the turning point, for better or worse, of an acute metaphorical disease. Moreover, the widespread crisis was made of interrelated specific points of pressure, which assumed material form at different times and in different places. As Stabb convincingly argues, the form was many times racial, but as this book will suggest, it could also be medical, geographical, sexual, political, and personal. Regardless of its form, for these writers, the Latin American crisis (metaphorical or material) was always a matter of fact.

In his book, Stabb tries to explain this tendency to call the state of the region a "sickness," and to ask repeatedly "why are we sick?" Stabb's explanation is both historical and psychological. He suggests that Latin Americans developed a defensiveness, and even an "inferiority complex," after the defeat of Spain in 1898 at the hands of the vigorous and ambitious Anglo-Saxon.[2] Thus weakened, he suggests, they were no match for "the vocabulary of the times." So, according to Stabb, Latin Americans blindly followed a rigid European scientific attitude, or "raciological analyses," whose "tenets have been proved erroneous."[3] They were dominated by positivism, "the philosophic embodiment" of that "scientific attitude."[4] They fell prey to movements that popularized and diffused biological thought such as Darwinism, social organicism, and the beginnings of physical anthropology.[5] Finally, Stabb suggests that they confused "metaphorical" and "provisional" approaches to the truth with the truth itself.[6]

Like the character of Settembrini in Thomas Mann's *Magic Mountain*, Stabb also sets the "decadence" of that pessimistic and "irrational scientism" against a progressive and modern "rational humanism." He argues that after this inauspicious beginning, Latin American writers rebelled against scientism. He states that the humanist rebellion had a "liberating effect." It broke the lugubrious imprisonment of positivism, refuted the "absolute value of the scientific fact," questioned "the blind faith in an absolute truth," asked for a degree of scientific skepticism, and placed science within its proper limits. He sees in humanism a philosophy that restores to Latin Americans in particular, and to mankind in general, that which positivism lost: the essentially human, the attention to the individual, and the notion of free will—all of which together offers the opportunity to act creatively and disinterestedly.

Stabb claims to belong to a cultural turn in the development of a Western humanist tradition. In Mexico, the "humanist rebellion" is dated 1908, when intellectual elites came together to form the famous "Athaeneum of Youth" (Ateneo de la Juventud). The members of the athaeneum set themselves apart from the earlier positivists, an action later described by Samuel Ramos as a "struggle against the demoralization produced by the Porfirian Era."[7] José Vasconcelos, another thinker belonging to this new humanism, described it historically, as the third social state in a Hegelian process of overcoming, subsuming, and transcending earlier states, defined respectively as overly materialistic and coldly intellectual.[8] Like Stabb, these humanists attempted to diagnose an "inferiority complex," or the "belief in the inferiority of the creole," which they believed was the result of the earlier knowledge or social state. They did so from a perspective other than the strictly biological approach of scientific positivism. Encompassing history, psychology, and social anthropology, the work of these humanists extended not only to Octavio Paz's influential *Labyrinth of Solitude* (1950), but has also appeared more recently in histories of medicine. Consider Noble David Cook's *Born to Die* (1988), for example, which suggests that the death and suffering people experienced through the pandemics during the conquest of the New World influenced their memory and self-representation.[9] Paradoxically, much of the humanist tradition ends up theorizing a notion of race, character, or identity based on essentialist assumptions, despite the supposed rebellion against a biological methodology and the embrace of a historical, psychological, or sociological perspective.

Is such humanism, then, truly "new"? Indeed, *Subjects of Crisis* seeks to problematize the so-called humanist rebellion. Stabb's argument rests on a notion of progress that drives many histories of ideas like his own. In his case, that notion is founded on the rejection of positivism and the embrace of a more ethical humanism. This progressive rejection, however, is belied by the continuities between the positivist assumptions he describes and his own humanist analysis. Consider that Stabb sets himself apart from the diagnosticians of sickness by characterizing positivism as a deterministic philosophy based on a scientific attitude. But he also claims that these diagnosticians suffered from an inferiority complex developed after a military defeat. What, then, is the difference between his diagnosis and theirs? Stabb may not be authorizing himself with anthroposociology, but he is similarly drawing from popular vocabulary and scientific knowledge. While Stabb's psychological assumptions did not seem "unfounded" to him, today the claims to authority of what Nikolas Rose has called "disciplines of psy" are very much in question.[10] And what about the supposed determinism of positivists? If biology plays no part in Stabb's humanist analysis, history seems to have inherited its overdetermining force. So, while anthroposociology and biology have disappeared from Stabb's humanist analysis, their explanatory force, or their authorizing function, has only shifted to new sciences; it has not disappeared.[11] Similarly, the shift has resulted in a metaphor for a "sick" people that is only slightly different from its nineteenth-century counterpart: instead of a racial disease suffered by the Latin American "masses," it is now an inferiority complex suffered by the diagnosticians themselves.

In this book, I presuppose the continuity between modern analyses like Stabb's and those of the diagnosticians of sickness at the turn of the century. Therefore, I cannot hold that the diagnosticians believed in sciences and knowledges that are clearly "outdated," "incorrect," or "unscientific," while Stabb's analysis is based on more "correct," "updated," or "truly scientific" knowledge. Neither do I believe that figurative use of language by the diagnosticians at the end of the century undermines the "truth" of their analyses, while Stabb's literal use of language makes his history of ideas more reliable.

Indeed, while it is true that Stabb gave crisis a literal meaning, and the diagnosticians used crisis figuratively, it is equally true that they both *saw* and *knew* crisis as a matter of fact. Neither Stabb nor the diagnosticians questioned the fact that a crisis existed, whether it was metaphorical or material.

How is it possible that crisis can perform the same authorizing function in opposite philosophies? What sustains the explanatory power of crisis for both positivists and humanists? I will attempt to explain how the factuality of those crises comes to be indisputable, in the face of changing standards of truth, and despite changes in what constitutes the evidence for truth. The indisputable and factual nature of crisis is, I will argue, the result of a network of histories, knowledges, and self-configurations; in other words, it is the effect of discourse.

Discourse, according to Michel Foucault, is a general term for what he also calls "exclusionary practices," which are key to understanding and self-understanding. While the term applies to linguistic events, discourse is not limited to them. Indeed, discourse is a network of interrelated, systematic, repeated, co-opting operations and performances of exclusion, which gives particular forms to perception and self-perception within disciplines, knowledges, and subjectivities. Thus, while the indisputable materiality of facts is the effect of discourse, discourse itself is not a matter of fact (in the traditional sense of "something that cannot be questioned," or the result of "plain common sense"). That is, discourse is not configured by ahistorical elements that could give it an intrinsically stable, coherent, material aspect. Instead, discourse is paradoxical. As Foucault puts it, while the explanatory power of discourse (its authorizing function) is "well known," its operations, impulses, and events are contradictory. Discourse seeks to both "gain mastery over its chance events," and "ward off its formidable materiality."[12] Neither is the repetitive nature of the operations of discourse the result of a conscious attempt or conspiracy to bias understanding or self-perception of a discipline, knowledge, or subjectivity. Indeed, many of the operations of discourse, as Foucault suggests, and as later Foucauldians like Judith Butler will have it, are unconscious.

Thus, while it may appear to be material in its effects, and figurative in its performances, discourse puts into question the very difference between matter and metaphor, fact and fiction, truth and error, and questions the existence of a world constituted solely by such binary oppositions. Discourse is a material operation at odds with its materiality, and a figurative representation uncomfortable with and even dismissive of its own figures. Discourse aims to be seen without being material. It wants to represent or signify without figures and without the mediation of signs. Discourse is not a matter of fact, but it aspires to be known and to be seen as a matter of fact. The distinction between fact and fiction is thus insufficient to explain discourse, and to understand it. Conversely, the presence of discourse in the world signals a world that is much more than the harmonious and coherent combination of similar sets of oppositions.[13]

Crisis, then, is a discourse. It can perhaps be visualized as a network, as a tense and malleable grid of exclusionary and coopting practices. Seeing, saying, and writing are all interrelated operations that help constitute this grid of perception and self-understanding. Figurative and scientific ideas, metaphors and facts, perception and emotion, all interact to produce something larger than their sum. They configure a knowledge that is not reducible to what is seen, but includes and mediates what is seen. Thus, to see is and can only be to see through, to face and be faced with, to be enveloped or masked by, a malleable grid made of competing self-conducted practices, many of which are unconscious. That self-produced mask, or membrane-like envelope, reaches both the gaze of the diagnosticians, and the crises of which they write.

So far, I have referred to a general tendency among these diagnosticians to represent Latin America as a region in crisis. Analyzing a specific example of this crisis might help me explain better what I mean when I say that to see and to know a crisis is to see through a discursive network.

How Is the Crisis Seen?

In hot pursuit of the cause of an apparently endemic anemic condition suffered by peasants in Puerto Rico, laboratory doctors anxiously followed the lead of Lieutenant Bailey K. Ashford. Ashford was a member of the military force that occupied the Caribbean island after the United States defeated the Spanish command that had governed the colony since 1493, in the Spanish-American War of 1898. Going against local medical practice, Ashford changed the focus of his investigations from the blood of his patients to the walls of their intestines. In his microscope, he saw the *Necator americanus*, a toothless version of an Old World hookworm (*Ancylostoma duodenale*). In his autobiography, Ashford maintains that he changed the focus of his medical gaze by chance. In *The Birth of the Clinic*, however, Foucault convincingly argues that such changes are not arbitrary; doctors look where they know to look. "The clinical gaze," he maintains, "is a perceptual act sustained by a logic of operations."[14] The medical gaze only "sees" a disease after it has classified it, after it has drawn its imaginary "picture," so to speak.

> Before it is removed from the density of the body, disease is given an organization, hierarchized into families, genera, and species. Apparently, this is no more than a "picture" that helps us to learn and to remember the proliferating domain

of the diseases. But at a deeper level than this spatial "metaphor," and in order to make it possible, classificatory medicine presupposes a certain "configuration" of disease: it has never been formulated for itself, but one can define its essential requisites after the event.[15]

Thus, Foucault might have argued that the shift in Ashford's field of vision, or medical (classificatory and clinical) gaze, was not arbitrary. Instead, following a slight shift in attention and concern from miscegenation to defilement and filth, Ashford decided to look at the patient's intestines rather than his blood. Ashford rejected the local doctors' "fantastic blood picture" in order to see the intestines of his patients. Ashford's rejection, Foucault would say, "is nothing more than a syntactical reorganization of disease in which the limits of the visible and invisible follow a new pattern."[16] This new pattern is determined by a shift in the doctor's concerns and anxieties; that shift, in turn, accompanies a change in the nature of the island's colonial relations. Miscegenation was a logical preoccupation for a population that occupied the island for four hundred years, and was anxious about the effect of racial mixing inside their own bodies. Filth and defilement were similarly logical concerns for a medico-military population that had only just arrived on the island, and whose notion of government would revolve around the concept of cleanliness.

In 1904, six years after the change in colonial administration, but only a short time after Ashford's "discovery," Quevedo Baez, a local doctor, looked into the same instrument and "saw" something quite different. As he reports in the February issue of the *Bulletin of the Medical Association of Puerto Rico*, Quevedo Baez "saw" a monster of fiction: a parasite ready to suck blood with its "mouth full of teeth and hooks." Local doctors were respected and powerful members of a professional and educated class; many of them were award-winning hygienists, trained in Paris, France. They occupied important positions in the government of the colony, before and after the Spanish-American War. Why did such a "scientific" group of men of medicine "see" such figures? One could argue with Stabb that their sophistication and scientific training were part of the problem. Stabb would argue that the "material" teeth and hooks they "saw" in the "mouth" of the parasite were, in fact, imaginary. They were the result of European racialist theories of disease that informed both their medical training and their colonial situation. A brief history of earlier configurations of the disease, however, suggests that the "teeth" and "hooks" were more than figurative.

After the successful slave revolts in Haiti (1791–1804), and by the middle of the nineteenth century, slaves (originally brought to the Spanish colony from the African continent) were, for many of the Spanish governor-generals of the island, the greatest threat to the future of the so-called Puerto Rican family. Echoing the concerns of the Spanish authorities, colonial doctors worried about the former slaves, who were free to "roam" the solitary jungles of the neglected colony after the abolition of slavery in 1873. They too believed that the newly-freed slaves threatened to contaminate the blood of the "white" peasant woman, constitutionally weakening her. As I argue in chapter 3, in their medical articles on miasma, they referred both to parasitic, vampire-like mosquitos and to invisible "populations," which infested the stagnant pools of water that produced the noxious fumes. Significantly, these visible mosquitos and invisible populations also polluted the blood of the "white" peasant woman in ways very similar to the threat posed by the "black" body. In these doctors' minds, parasitic mosquitos, invisible jungle populations, and "black" bodies, were all agents of the same anemic condition. Indeed, mosquitos and "black" bodies were collapsed into the same material, contaminating category through the intervention of the figurative invisible population. In this way, material mosquitos became metaphors for, or came to represent, the "black" body. Matter and metaphor collapsed to configure anemia, an event that went beyond matter and metaphor. Anemia was a discourse that naturalized a presupposed difference between "races." By collapsing a "black race" into the image of an insect contaminating the blood of the "white" peasant woman, local doctors fixed the difference between "blacks" and "whites" on the material hook of the mosquito. For the laboratory doctors of tropical medicine, such discrete biological evidence was a more convincing measure of the difference between the "races" than skin color could ever be.[17]

Ashford's move away from blood did nothing to assuage the local doctors' well-established fear of miscegenation. In fact, the toothless version of the hookworm amounted to a virtual rejection of a racial divide that was as plainly visible to the doctors as a difference in color. The hooks were the result of a discursive network or grid that ordered knowledge and perception according to the matter, the metaphors, and the fears that constituted it. The fear of racial difference, thus, was built into the grid that configured the local doctors' gaze. Fear helped to constitute the act of looking itself, making it impossible for them to look away from a racial threat. There was nothing else on which they could fix their gaze, if not the parasite's hooks and teeth. They neither imagined nor consciously made up those teeth and hooks. Rather, they saw material evidence that confirmed a material difference between the races. Thus, even after colonial relations were reconfigured, the doctors held on to the hooks of earlier configurations of the discourse of anemia.

The effects of that gaze were equally material. It led them to the inevitable conclusion that the blood of the peasant woman had to be protected. Her body had to be managed and her movement controlled in order to neutralize the racialized threat. Their perception and understanding of the disease led them to a treatment that was different from Ashford's. He treated anemia with a pill that would get rid of the worm, while the local doctors preferred to oversee the movement, and govern the conduct, of racialized bodies in crisis through broader types of intervention such as health education. The local doctors' adjustment to the picture of the parasite and their alternative treatment suggest that a discourse excludes and co-opts competing discourses, or the discourses at its margins. The negotiations and adjustments between the local medical discourses and those of their metropolitan counterparts bear out Foucault's claim that there is no one ruling discourse. This is particularly true of situations of changing colonial relations, where there is a constant struggle between competing discourses, and a constant repositioning of competing discourses from the margins to the center of the conflict.

All of the chapters of this book presuppose the existence of discursive networks such as anemia, and describe the changes brought about by the competition between discourses in the colonial context that configures Latin America. Of the book's five chapters, the first focuses on the analysis and description of such networks. It looks at the mapping practices of European and Americans who traveled through the region of what is today Colombia and Venezuela, from the end of the eighteenth to the middle of the nineteenth centuries. Those mapping practices are examples of discursive networks. In that chapter, I examine competing maps of figurative landscapes and bodyscapes, and I describe their material effect.

As the title of chapter 1 suggests, "Walking Backward to the Future" presupposes a second fundamental concept organizing this book. Unlike Stabb, who sees history as a linear progressive flow of events whose force overdetermines the diagnosis of sickness, I see history as a layered series of sustained events with timelines that sometimes are parallel, sometimes intersect, and sometimes loop back on themselves. Discourse (knowledge, self-knowledge, and subjectivity) is historical in the sense that it is also (but *not* mainly) the result of these timelines, or layered series of events. Thus, while discourse is intrinsically unstable and contradictory, it is always made of practices that are not linear, but temporal. Such temporal layers configure the landscapes and bodyscapes mapped by the local members of the traveling expeditions discussed in the first chapter. But these layered histories also configure the particular and familiar shape of the travelers themselves, and of all of the subjects of this book.

What Are the Histories of Crisis?

Many of the subjects on whom I focus in this book saw themselves as racialized and virile subjects. Racial and sexual difference mattered to them in a specific way. The changes brought about by the general and particular histories of racial and sexual difference were, for them, a matter of fact. In short, they saw themselves as creole *letrados*, to borrow a term from Angel Rama.[18] He uses it to describe not only a class of cultured intellectuals, but also a particular type of colonized consciousness. Such a consciousness accepts as matters of fact the arbitrary connections between signs and referents produced in the contested zone of contact between a metropolitan discourse of occupation, the discourses that predated it, and the discourses that emerge after the metropolitan forces arrive. In other words, it is a consciousness that has interiorized racialized and gendered discourses, but also uses them to their best advantage. Thus, creole *letrados* saw themselves as educated *white men* of Spanish ancestry, but born in the colonies. Conversely, they saw their responsibility as managing a body differently racialized and gendered from their own: the anemic body of the peasant woman, and the "black" body of supposed members of an "African race," in the case of the *letrados* from Puerto Rico.

To understand the *letrado*'s self-configuration, it helps to historicize it. My aim in doing so is not to reduce subjectivity to history, but to help discourse take apart its own "formidable materiality." To historicize, then, does not mean to inscribe subjectivity into one historical line. It is, instead, to turn matters of fact into temporal layers, or histories, that sometimes follow distinct timelines, and sometimes intersect. To return to our specific example, the subjectivity of the *letrado* and the associated shape of its "charge" are the result of a local history of political struggle for autonomy. They exist within the context of Puerto Rico's colonization.

In 1898, approximately six years before Quevedo Baez "saw" and wrote about the parasite's teeth, and after decades of political struggle, the *letrados* on that island reached a negotiated solution with the Spanish authorities that gave them autonomy in government. The history of this struggle for autonomy partly explains the held-over teeth of a microscopic parasite. As I argue in more detail in chapter 3, the *letrados* empowered themselves against the local Spanish bureaucrats by mollifying their counterparts overseas. They configured themselves against a "black" body of an "African race." In this way, *letrados* rejected the way the local Spanish authorities configured them; they reconfigured themselves. In 1904, six years after this negotiated solution had been reached, those same *letrados* found themselves back at square one, so to speak, engaged in a similar process of negotiation with a different metropolitan authority. The return of the familiar teeth and hooks to the new site of the parasite would be one outcome of such negotiations.

But the loops in the political history of sustained struggle between a metropolitan authority and a colonized subject are ultimately insufficient to explain the particular form taken by the parasite. Why, for example, the particular concern with blood-sucking represented by the hooks and teeth, and by the mosquitos that preceded them? To explain this concern, one must go to a parallel layer: the appropriation of competing knowledge that is indigenous, rather than metropolitan, in nature. While such appropriations take place in the same zone of contact, they have their own history. Some of these appropriations date back at least five hundred years to the encounter of a Spanish shipwrecked sailor called Cabeza de Vaca with local medical practitioners, who he learned to impersonate in order to survive. Others, like the vampire after which the fanged parasite is modeled, are the result of local popular imagery appropriated by the doctors in order to compete with the local medical practice of midwives.

Moreover, race was medicalized in those temporal and spatial zones of contact. The history of that medicalization is also relevant to the specific shape of Quevedo Baez's parasite, because that history is abundant in examples of similar visualizations. Helped by parallel acquisition of ethnographic, anthropological, geographic, and sociological knowlege, first clinical medicine and later the laboratory and tropical medicine of the nineteenth and twentieth centuries configured differentiated disease networks. These networks made distinctions between diseases like anemia, yellow fever, goiter, epilepsy, criminal insanity, and degeneration not only epidemiologically, but also by linking them to specific races and places. The local doctors' interest in miasma and mosquitos, and their anxiety about blood and race, are examples of the fixed coordinates that helped to configure the teeth in the mouth of the parasite. Conversely, the biological distance that the *letrados* "saw" between their "white," "European-like" body, and the body of the similarly "white" peasant woman, depended on their successful redrawing of the boundaries of those discoursive networks.

The attention to these local and general histories, however, is still insufficient to explain the parasite's singular attraction to the body of the peasant *woman*, and the doctors' self-configuration as *virile* medical subjects. To better hold the monster by its teeth, as it were, the history of the configuration of subjectivity must engage with another timeline: the history of its virility. Doctors like Quevedo Baez, Francisco del Valle Atiles, or the well-known naturalist novelist Manuel Zeno Gandía, understood themselves in opposition to what was, for them, the evidently dangerous disruptive and hysterical nature of a sexually different body. Midwives and peasant and urban women were all "seen" as natural bodies in biological crisis that had to be ordered and managed for their own good. Kelly Oliver has traced the history of this particular discoursive struggle that pits a natural female body against a social male body from contemporary philosophy back to classical forms.[19] She has persuasively argued that this history leads the resulting subjectivity into a self-fulfilling paradox: a subject confused, and handicapped, by the very gendered discourses of struggle and domination that configure it. The *letrado* will not escape the consequences of its similar historical configuration as a subject driven by domination and struggle, as we will see.

Thus, crisis is the result of a series of parallel, intersecting, and sometimes repeating, timelines. The series includes the history of political empowerment, of localized struggle, of broad contact between populations and empires, of the medicalization of race, and of the virilization of subjectivity. All of the chapters in this book engage with one, or with several, of these layered histories. But chapters 2 and 3 are perhaps the most ambitious in this regard, casting the broadest historical net. In chapter 2, "Weaning the Virile Subject," I describe the genealogy of a virile and racialized Creole subjectivity. In it, I examine the works of Colombian writers who followed in the steps of the travelers of the first chapter, reaching different levels of self-configuration, and Other-formation. In chapter 3, "Anemia, Witches, and Vampires," I describe a different genealogy of the same virile and racialized Creole subjectivity. In that chapter, I emphasize the effects that subjectivity suffers from a repeating loop in the history of colonization. One of the effects of that loop is the third and final fundamental concept informing this book.

Chapter 3 ends with a meditation on the processes that force a child to see himself differently. It traces, and interprets, the pained expression in the subject's young face as the child interiorizes the nightmarish vision offered him by the laboratory doctor, as he becomes an Other to himself. Significantly, this process of interiorization affects not only the configured Other, but also the configuring Self. This process, which I also call a self-violence, is the turn inward of that nightmarish vision for the specific purpose of constituting subjectivity. The self-violence at the center of similar processes of self-configuration is the third and final concept that organizes this book.

Who Is the Subject of Crisis?

The *letrado* is the result not only of a triumphant sustained history of violent, reactionary oppositions and conflicts. In fact, the *letrado*'s liberal, reform-minded practices are the result also of a history of selections, cooptations, cannibalizations, transculturations, and adjustments. Indeed, *letrados* saw themselves as different from their predecessors because of these less direct, more functional and dynamic responses to alternative and competing knowledges, disciplines, and subjectivities. They made the necessary adjustments to the contradictions of believing both in the theological principle of unity gleaned from Scripture, and in the scientific principle of deviation learned from the theory of degeneration. They produced the required interpretations to reconcile a world view organized by racial hierarchy with their own racial mixture. They adjusted their way of government to balance competing imperial and republican ideals. They appropriated the strategies of resistance that the indigenous collectivities opposed to their governing practices.

The price of this particular kind of subjectivity, however, proved to be rather high. If discursive practices have a way of turning against themselves in the most surprising ways, those of the educated elites of *letrados* were certainly no exception. The liberal impulse that shifted the methods of control away from direct confrontation with alternative discourses led to internal methods of control whose long-lasting problematic consequences Rose describes in his recent work on modern self-invention.[20] He convincingly argues that the modern Self emerges from the intersection of government (or the administration of human resources) and what he calls the "psy" sciences (or the intellectual technology that makes visible previously invisible "inner" spaces). Rose's fascinating meditation on the consequences of such self-configuration owes much to Friedrich Nietzsche's philosophical analysis of the "bad conscience."

> This instinct for freedom forcibly made latent . . . this instinct for freedom pushed back and repressed, incarcerated within and finally able to discharge and vent itself only on itself: that, and that alone, is what the bad conscience is in its beginnings.[21]

As Nietzsche argues in his famous diatribe against Christian morality and values, the turn inward of "discipline" and "surveillance" is not simply a substitution of old-fashioned order from above, with modern self-configuration. Rather, the turn is an adjustment in, and it is in continuity with, an age-old system of morality that Nietzsche sets out to demystify. Neither is the interiorization of the "instinct for freedom" a sign of progress, as the *letrados* would have us believe. It is not the substitution of a repressive system of belief with a modern secular one based on the individual's freedom. Instead, that interiorization is a clear sign of a self-violence, which Nietzsche calls degeneration, ironically mimicking the physiologists, but also bringing attention to the body that they want to escape. "Bad conscience," or the turn inward of the violence that Nietzsche calls the "instinct for freedom," leads to selves that are eager to lose their worldly shell. The turn of the "will to power" against the Self explains the unconscious attraction felt by the *letrado* to see more clearly, to get closer, to the perceived source of its own death. The *letrado*'s configuration is not different from the modern Self described by Rose. The *letrado* emerges extremely preoccupied with normality, and is therefore prone to self-interrogation. He emerges as a subject of crisis, afraid of himself, and ready to do anything to put a safe distance between himself and the internalized object of his deepest fears. He also emerges ready to see a "mouth full of teeth and hooks" inside a subject of crisis, a mouth that terrorizes him, and that he significantly *desires* to control.

We find this turn of the Self against itself in all of the chapters of this book. But it is most apparent in chapters 4 and 5. In chapter 4, "Crossing the Boundaries of Madness," I show that the effort of Argentinean criminologist José Ingenieros to describe insanity scientifically, and to exclude figurative language from his own discourse, is more than a strategy to configure a discipline. It is also a practice of self-configuration that ends up crossing the very boundaries it sets for itself. Similarly, in chapter 5, "The Crisis of Memory," I describe a self-violence that is necessary for self-configuration, but this time in the work of two novelists living at the turn of the century in different countries. In the works of all of these writers, self-violence is revealed to be a technique of self-configuration.

Subjects of Crisis

As should be clear from this introduction, the organization of this book is principally conceptual. It traces three forms of the same configuration, which I have attempted to describe here, namely the discursive and historical configuration of crisis, and the violent configuration of a subject of crisis. In other words, the book attempts to trace the complex operations and the genealogy of discourses of Self and Other in Latin America. It also describes the changing spatial landscapes, the critical bodyscapes, and the conflicting histories that configure that region. Its aim is to tease a kinship out of these particular configurations of region, Self, and Other, a kinship found in the nature of the contests between the knowledges and the disciplines constituting them. The book also attempts to balance the similarity of these discursive processes of configuration with the significant differences in the subjectivities, knowledges, and disciplines at stake. These similarities in the processes, and the differences in the points of departure and arrival, hint at the complexities governing race and gender in Latin America. They suggest the need for creative interpretation, for "dancing lightly on one's feet" as Nietzsche might have put it, in the attempt to understand them better.

The organization of the book is also loosely chronological and geographical. Chapter 1 discusses works that date as far back as the end of the eighteenth century. Chapters 4 and 5 discuss works written during the first two decades of the twentieth century. It also covers much geographical ground, including works published in, and about, Colombia, Venezuela, Argentina, and Puerto Rico. The list of characters involved in the drama it seeks to tell is equally diverse: it includes imperial European travelers, military capitalist entrepreneurs, military doctors, Americanized Europeans, statesmen or patrician *letrados*, younger professional *letrados*, *cargueros*, midwives, and so on.

The first act of this drama, or dance, opens with the changes in the mapping practices, or fictions of time and race, by Alexander Humboldt and

Agustín Codazzi. I interpret the output of their enterprises as different discoursive grids ordering space and time, and giving different structure and order to bodies in conflict. I describe the passing of an incongruous metropolitan subject, a lofty European traveler, and his imperial gaze. I also underscore a shift away from his mapping practices, his ideal landscapes that erase the danger of the Other. And I end by recording the emergence of an inchoate, self-critical, colonial subjectivity: a hybrid subject that rehearses a more practical mapping practice that meets the changing needs of a republican form of government. The practice, however, while promising self-government, is also based on the problematic principle of self-removal.

In the second act, I trace a connection between gender and crisis at the center of a metaphorical network set up to make a collective body visible and governable, and to construct a virile subjectivity. I argue that in a political essay by José M. Samper, and in the well-known novel by Jorge Isaacs, reproduction stands for the principles of duality and difference. It stands for the threat of decapitation, the threat to the principles of unity and singularity. Reproduction stands for crisis itself. Thus, Samper, in his work, consciously refers to his essays as a masculine act of knowledge or analysis, and refers to the history of Colombia's political crises as a sustained feminine act of reproduction.

I then go on to interpret Isaacs's novel as a similar identification of the body of women with a health crisis of national dimensions, and with its political consequences. If blood, or the feminine body, is at the center of the inherited crisis, Isaacs argues that analysis by a masculine mind is the exercise necessary to overcome it.

I conclude by pointing out that the works by these writers also imagine a disembodied Creole Self trying to govern a decapitated Other. In other words, their discursive networks produce a paradoxical and ungovernable set of subjectivities. More specifically, what I refer to in my analysis as "the *letrado's* logic of singularity" is called into question by what the *letrado* admits to be a critical point of origin. In his attempt to overcome this problem, the *letrado* abandons and separates himself from this point of origin, and succeeds in configuring himself instead with a nostalgic discourse based on absolute loss and radical rupture.

Chapter 3 focuses on the construction of anemia as an endemic disease by Creole intellectuals during the last two decades of the nineteenth century. Focusing on the medical and sociological debates about anemia, I trace the nationalist use of such phantasms and their location within the body of the "white" peasant woman. A group of Creole intellectuals, bent on negotiating power with a force of occupation, cannibalize the ruling scientific paradigms, manipulate nonscientific and convenient popular imagery, and finally interiorize a normative state of crisis, in their effort to appoint themselves authoritative technical administrators of an island they perceive to be diseased.

In chapter 4, I discuss the construction of the concept of a normative state of crisis or insanity in the psychological literature of the turn of the century. I also underscore the debt owed by scientific discourse to figurative language even as scientists have denied that debt. Scientific discourse depends on metaphor both to make the crisis visible and to prevent a universalization of the crisis that would turn on the scientific discourse itself. Rigorous description of the normative state of crisis inevitably brings the doctor and the insane closer together, and leads to implications that do not escape the psychologists.

Chapter 4 focuses on the change in scientific paradigms that occurred at the turn of the century, when the budding science of psychology shifted from a morphological concern with location of lesions in the brain mass to a functional approach. I focus on the works of two major Argentinean psychologists: José María Ramos Mejía and José Ingenieros.

In chapter 5, I describe the paradox that results from the attempt to know and govern the Self: the necessary inscription, or infolding, of crisis into the fabric of the Self. The attempt to know ourselves, to make ourselves knowable, leads to a necessary violence. It reduces and disciplines an intersubjective, infinite, and timeless becoming.

In this final act, I discuss two such gestures of subjectification that turn becoming into different mnemonic devices: a *camera obscura* and a magic lantern. These devices work in different ways and result in different subjects. If the first operates as a hollowing out process, the second operates instead by layering. If the first produces a consciousness, the second results in an unconscious, as is suggested by my study of the only novel by the well-known modernist from Colombia José Asunción Silva.

I also argue, however, that the same gestures that turn becoming into a hallowed I, also turn it into either a hollow grave or a funerary urn. Either way, the subjecting process that constructs and aims to govern a knowable self results, instead, in a liquidated and ungovernable Self.

1

Walking Backward to the Future

TIME, TRAVEL, AND RACE

A violent blow to the head removed me from the contemplative mood
inspired by the sublime natural spectacle. The scene's only drawback was
the ridiculous way in which it appeared, for I saw it as we walked away.
The blow made me start with fright. I disobeyed the explicit instructions of
the carrier, who had warned me against any sudden movement. The
carguero reproached me and stumbling on his three feet said:
—Don't even think of it, young master.
—Even if you kill me?
—Not for the moment, *blanco*! But we hit a head-bender.
—It seemed more like a neck-breaker to me.
The *carguero* ignored my angry reprimand, pretending he had not heard
it, bent over, and brought us safely from under the proverbial yoke.
—Santiago Pérez, Museo de Cuadros de Costumbres

Introduction

The passage describes a popular means of travel by *carguero*[1] between the
two Colombian cities of Ibagué and Cártago through the Quindío mountain
pass at two thousand five hundred meters above sea level. Part "colored" and
part "white," part "barbarian" and part "civilized," placed at the crossroads of

the fourteenth and the nineteenth centuries, the dramatization of the composite figure of the *carguero* and its white burden stands in Santiago Pérez's travel account as an allegorical representation of fictions of time and race constructed throughout the nineteenth century.

The composite figure is represented stumbling toward the future while looking back at the past. The sequence from the self-absorbed contemplation of a primitively sublime nature, to the violent blow to the head, the stumbling carrier, and the final implied threat, censures the mystification of the *viajero encumbrado*, the lofty European traveler who revels in his visions of a utopian relationship between different races and different times. The threat of a material fall warns the reader of the reification of the "mapping" practices of such travelers. It alerts the reader to the pitfalls of constructing ideal maps in order to rule over a threatening landscape by merely fixing and articulating its temporal and racial coordinates.

The passage instead hints at a topsy-turvy world where the coordinates fixed by such mapping practices are in carnivalesque disarray. In contrast to the traveler's contemplation of an eternal nature, the writer calls attention to the sudden awareness of the traveler's mortality. Likewise the freedom of his backward glance is abruptly curtailed by the realization of his actual state. The traveler realizes that he must abide by an unwritten law of immobility laid down by the *carguero* if he is to survive. This knowledge puts him in an uncomfortable position: he must not move, he must resign himself to a lack of agency, if he is to survive the trip. In this way his apparent superiority is contradicted by his submission to the law of the *carguero*, whose flippant response suggests that he is well aware of the ironic position in which the traveler finds himself. Indeed, the playful death threat and the *carguero's* forward movement underscore both his own agency and his knowledge of the real coordinates of the landscape around him. The *carguero* is aware of the fact that in a critical moment the life of the traveler above him is metaphorically in his hands, and literally at his feet. The passage dramatizes a dystopia where the slave has become the master.[2]

The figure of the *carguero* appears in many Colombian travel narratives throughout the nineteenth century, where it is often accompanied by striking illustrations. It was the subject of one of the sights described in Alexander Humboldt's *Researches Concerning the Institutions and Monuments of the Ancient Inhabitants of America*, first published in 1810.[3] It was also described in the travel narratives of the "capitalist vanguard"[4] that followed in Humboldt's steps.[5] Finally, it appeared in the travel accounts of the South American educated elite, or letrados,[6] such as Santiago Pérez.[7]

Perhaps the *carguero* was ubiquitous because it cut such a striking figure. On the one hand, its composite nature included both the narrating Self and the described Other, presenting an opportunity to discuss colonial relations much as Pérez did. On the other hand, its representation of social inequality often led the travelers to ethical reflections. In fact, many European travelers reacted like Humboldt, expressing a sense of moral outrage at the sight of such apparent inequality. Such a response would set the European account apart from that of the Euro-American *letrado* were it not for the fact that the careful reader detects in the European response the same anxiety felt by Pérez. Such fear riddles all of the travel narratives. It comes from an awareness of the precariousness of the master-slave diad suggested by the composite figure. "Indeed, an oft-recounted story [by European travelers] concerns an otiose official spurring on his *sillero*, who became so angry that he bent forward and hurled his tormentor into the abyss below."[8]

While the educated *letrado* resigned himself to riding on the back of his temporary master, many of the European travelers refused the ride. And yet, while travelers like Humboldt idealistically claimed that they kept fast to their decision, many European travelers confessed to overcoming their initial repulsion. Those who eventually mounted the *carguero* did so with great moral reservations; many continued to complain about the inhumanity of the practice in which they were engaging. All rode the *carguero* very carefully, trying to sleep or to read a book, "keeping absolutely still lest the *sillero* fall."[9]

The differences and similarities in the responses to the *carguero* point to important variations in colonial relations over time and across collectivities. They hint at ruptures and continuities between the different stabilizing projects and mapping practices of Humboldt, the "capitalist vanguard," and the *letrados*. These adjustments to changing colonial relations are the focus of this chapter.

Perez's allegory is found in the dispersed travel notes from his tenure as the official chronicler of Colombia's famous Chorography Commission.[10] The travel notes are part of a work that appears to modern readers to be constituted by a number of "closed and apparently autonomous nuclei"[11] because it was never assembled into a multivolume set, as were the works of Humboldt, for example.[12] The works of the Chorography Commission were probably intended to appear as a multivolume set. As in the case of Humboldt, the name that heads the collective enterprise, Agustín Codazzi, became synonymous with the commission itself, and it was expected that a single work under his name would emerge.

In fact, the commission itself owed much to earlier voyages like Humboldt's five-year expedition to the Americas. Like Humboldt, Codazzi did not travel alone, and his texts put together pieces of knowledge from different contributors. Like Humboldt's expedition, the Chorography Commission extended over a number of years, and drew from such varied disciplines as geography, botany, ethnography, and literature. Moreover, the commission also produced physical descriptions, geographic and statistical charts, reports, descriptions of manners and customs, and plates of the sights and sites "seen" by the travelers.

The difference in the fate befalling the texts produced by each enterprise, however, remains significant. It suggests that the maps and texts produced both by the collective enterprise that was Humboldt's, and by the Chorography Commission, were different stages in the attempt to construct a discoursive grid ordering both space and time.[13] Put in another way, Humboldt's expedition and Codazzi's commission were both attempts to fix the spatial frontiers and temporal boundaries of imagined communities, but they were attempts to imagine them differently.[14] Indeed, Codazzi's commission represented an adjustment in these versatile mapping practices, which met the changing needs of a republican form of government steadily moving away from centralized discipline and surveillance.[15] (The change is evident even in the unfamiliar word *chorography*, which means the art or practice of describing, or of delineating on a map or chart, particular regions or districts—as distinct from geography, which deals with the earth in general, and topography, which deals with particular places.) Moreover, the move from Humboldt to Codazzi was also the result of a change in the point of enunciation: from an incongruous metropolitan subject bent on keeping order in its colonies to an inchoate colonial subject trying its hand at self-discipline. These combined differences account for the fragmentary nature of Codazzi's text, and for the unitary nature of Humboldt's. How they do so is the subject of the following sections.

Humboldt's Cosmic Time and Temporal Scarcity

Critics have argued that one of Humboldt's principal discursive strategies was "to reduce America to landscape and marginalize its inhabitants."[16] Consequently, his I/eye has been fixed at the crossroad of conflicting informational and experiential discourses. According to these critics, from this position Humboldt prepares a fantasy of dominance, or what has been called the strategy of the monarch that surveys all.[17] But Humboldt's works also diagnose the breakdown of that monumental subject. Indeed, they stand as monuments to the consequences of gargantuan imperial conflict and overextension.

Born in Berlin in 1769, Humboldt had witnessed events catastrophic to the Prussian monarchy: the crossing of the Rhine by Revolutionary French troops in 1792, the surrender of the Austrian Netherlands and Brussels in the Battle of Valmy (1792), and the dismemberment of the Holy Roman Empire in 1806. It was in fact the Napoleonic Wars in Egypt, Syria, and Italy, fought against the Prussian and Ottoman empires, that radically changed Humboldt's travel plans six times between 1797 and 1799, and postponed his departure to regions whose charm was overdetermined by his youthful fantasies. Moreover, Humboldt began writing his *Personal Narrative of Travels to the Equinoctial Regions of the New Continent during the Years 1799–1804*[18] in 1813, a year that marked the limits of three European empires: the French, overextended and waging war on two fronts, the British, at war with its former colonies, and the Spanish, involved in an ill-fated struggle to maintain its own. Indeed, Humboldt represented even the wars between empires and their colonies as monumental struggles between civilizing imperial monarchs and a savage natural empire, each claiming the inchoate colonies of the equinoctial regions as its own.

Thus, Humboldt's imperial fictions emerge as precarious attempts to map, order, and extend the frontiers of empires in singular disarray. The precariousness of these frontiers is revealed by Humboldt's discourse on time and space. On the one hand, desiring an orderly world free from conflict, he set out to find temporal analogies among empires, indeed among continents and races, that seemed to his contemporaries to be terribly distant from one another.[19] On the other hand, Humboldt was seduced by the romantic rhythm of dying empires, and by the nostalgic pleasure of writing a personal narrative of his travels, even as he felt afraid of those same revolutionary rhythms, and of the resulting rupture with his own past. These fears and desires set free in his narrative the anxieties of a wandering subject far from his disintegrating country and increasingly aware of his own mortality.

Together with these domestic and personal concerns about empire and revolution, Humboldt's works also voiced a great interest in, and a concern about, the existence and agency of an American Other. Like many of his contemporary travelers, following the romantic ideal of a union between subject and cosmos, Humboldt drew ever closer to an American subject that he helped to shape. As the gap between subject and object narrowed, Humboldt tried to keep his scientific distance with classifications and taxonomies, and felt the force of the resistant Other rebelling against those mapping practices. These struggles resulted in what González Echevarría has insightfully described as an asymptote between subject and object, which further turned the expedition to the Americas into a voyage of self-discovery.[20]

Perhaps the most emblematic moment of Humboldt's efforts to map a monumental and even cosmic time, to fix the coordinates between imperial Europe and colonial America, takes place at the beginning of his *Personal Narrative*, as he attempts to map the temporal boundaries of his own life.[21] It is a moment significantly marked by time, space, and loss. Always projecting maps onto his travels, Humboldt fixes the otherwise permeable boundary between the temperate zone of Europe and the torrid zone of the Americas with a reference to the celestial maps of Flamstead and La Caille. Sailing through the Atlantic Ocean, Humboldt fixes for the reader the location of the equinoctial regions with their "exotic" constellations. More important, he compares a constellation like the Southern Cross to a celestial clock regularly recording time with its rotation. Like the maps, the Southern Cross brings distant peoples and places together because it is a reference point for both Europeans and Americans.[22] It gives Humboldt and his readers a sense of order when faced with an unfamiliar sky.

But if the Southern Cross stands for a cosmic time bringing distant people together, it also stands for Humboldt's past. It confronts him with the original impulse for his trip: the desire to fulfill the dreams of his youth.[23] The cross then becomes a different kind of clock for Humboldt. It no longer represents an eternity that incorporates different peoples and places; now it represents temporal scarcity. Humboldt meditates on the short time remaining to fulfill his dreams, and appropriately ends the passage with a reference to an epidemic fever that suddenly threatens all the travelers on board. The fevers paradoxically bring the reader back to Humboldt's stabilizing mapping practices because they are a fixed coordinate. Disease marks both changes in temperature and the proximity to the torrid zone, whose heat (according to the medical knowledge of the time) could be fatal if experienced too rapidly by the European traveler.

This complex network of time and space reveals a work at odds with itself. The tension is most poignant in the fears and hopes that drive Humboldt's writing. Like the monuments themselves, Humboldt's descriptions are "memorials of history." He takes his time with every step of the journey, exhaustively developing each coordinate of the cosmic nexus he is mapping (the first 240 pages of the *Personal Narrative* describe the preparation for the trip and the passage to the equinoctial region.) And he is aware of the ideological importance of such maps. He argues that the collective memory that once kept empires together has been lost to distance and climate. The people of the colonies have forgotten not only the past of the metropolis but their own past as well, and that double loss has separated the colonies and the metropolis from each other.[24] To write about that past is to bring them back together, to preserve the tenuous link between the colonial and the metropolitan space.

But to write is also to postpone hopelessly a desired end. The monuments and their descriptions are obstacles delaying Humboldt and separating him from his future projects, making it impossible to enjoy his present. "Haunted by the fear of not executing the designs of the morrow," Humboldt lives and writes "in perpetual uneasiness."[25] The imposing size of the temporal bridge, of the monumental past history, with which Humboldt means to bring the colonies and the metropolis back together, is belied by his awareness of its precariousness. Humboldt knows that his monumental narrative is boring; it has been pointed out that he had grown so bored of the project that he abandoned it before it was finished. But perhaps it was not only boredom that kept Humboldt from finishing his project; perhaps he did not have time to finish his project, stimulated by the sight of old regimes coming to an end, and by his youthful desire to fulfill all of his dreams before it was too late.

Ideal Landscapes and Bodyscapes

Catering to the modern and commercial subject that speeds through his text saying "forget the past and show me the future," Humboldt writes his widely popular *Researches, Concerning the Institutions and Monuments of the Ancient Inhabitants of America, with Descriptions and Views of the Most Striking Scenes in the Cordilleras!* A different kind of book from the *Personal Narrative, Researches* is a collection of "greatest hits," or perhaps an early form of the brochures now found at travel agencies. It elegantly adjusts itself to the modern reader's quickening pace, while preserving a reduced version of the complex network of discourses about time and space. As such it packs a more powerful punch than *Personal Narrative*.

In the introduction to *Researches*, Humboldt argued for a temporal and physical continuity between the so-called old and new continents. For Humboldt, the American continent was older than had been previously thought and its landscape was as ancient as Europe's.[26] Geological catastrophes were global, as were the migrations of species and races. Accordingly, the fables, myths, and even the conception of time of the ancient inhabitants of the American continent were similar to those of the Etruscans, the Egyptians, and the Tibetans. Even if it was "cut off from the rest of mankind" and was far from the Greek and Roman race, the American race, Humboldt argued, bore a striking resemblance to the races of the "old" continent, specifically to the race of the "Mongol nations."

This temporal, spatial, and racial continuity is perhaps best expressed by the plates that accompanied the book, and in particular by Humboldt's striking illustration of the *carguero* crossing the mountain pass of the Quindío (fig. 1).[27] The plate suggests further differences with the *Personal Narrative*. It modifies the imperial perspective of *Personal Narrative,* which maps time and space and fixes their coordinates. At first, the gaze composing the plate seems organized by a series of opposites encompassing all time and space. With one visual gesture it fixes the past and the future, the near and the far, the high and the low, all of which have familiar meanings attached: civilization and barbarism, life and death, city and jungle. Slightly off to one side of the central composite figure, however, stands a *carguero,* whose empty chair

Fig. 1. *Passage of Quindu, in the Andes Mountain Range.* Drawing by Koch in Rome, based on a sketch by Humboldt. Engraved by Duttenhofer in Stuttgard. In Alexander Humboldt, *Atlas pittoresque du voyage: Vues des Cordillères, et monumens des peuples indigènes de a'Amérique* (Amsterdam: Theatrum Orbus Terrarum Ltd.; and New York: Plenum Publishing Corporation, (1971–1972), vol. 7, plate 5. The Hague, Koninklijke Biblitheek.

and glance reorganize the plate's composition. On the one hand, the empty chair is a visual cue for Humboldt's equalizing gestures. The reader of *Researches* knows that Humboldt has refused to ride on his *carguero*. On the other hand, the second *carguero* moves the monarch's gaze away from the first *carguero*, and looks back at him, substituting the original binomial pattern of hierarchies with a triangular composition.

The plate not only moves the gaze through space, from the first to the second *carguero*, it also suggests a temporal move between the same *carguero* at different moments in time. And indeed, both figures are identical except for one thing. The second *carguero*, now free from his burden, but keeping his position, looks up and out of the picture plane, as if acknowledging the change. Humboldt's concern with the sight of a *carguero* carrying a traveler on his back seems to make the body of the traveler magically disappear from the chair of a second *carguero*. The glance transports the disembodied presence of the traveler outside the picture plane, making it occupy the same space as the monarch. The combined gaze of both the tourist and the monarch then rests at the peak of a triangular composition whose base is formed by the two *cargueros*, and by a temporal dynamic that sets the *carguero* in motion and propels the traveler higher up. The new composition suggests a firmer base for the paternal monarchy, founded on the ideal of equality among siblings (not between parent and child). But it also modifies the hierarchy represented by the composite figure of the *carguero* front and center, by permitting the coincidence of traveler and monarch in the same space. And finally, it apparently safely moves everyone a step forward, figuratively advancing everyone's best interests by promoting equality between the *carguero* and the traveler, and by opening up the privileged gaze of the monarch to the bourgeois tourist.

The complexity of the plate's composition is enhanced by an idealization of the figure of the *carguero* in the text. Unlike the *carguero* front and center, the second *carguero* and the abstracted traveler exchange glances. The narrative develops this exchange into a meaningful identification.

> They talk in this country of going on a man's back (*andar en carguero*), as we mention going on horseback, no humiliating idea is annexed to the trade of car-gueroes; and the men who follow this occupation are not Indians, but mulattoes, and sometimes even whites . . . When we reflect on the enormous fatigue to which these miserable men are exposed . . . ; when we know that their backs are sometimes raw as those of beasts of burden, and that travelers have often the cruelty to leave them in the forests . . . ; that they earn by a journey from Ibague to Carthago only twelve or fourteen piasters . . . ; we are at a loss to conceive, how this employment of a carguero . . . is eagerly embraced by all the robust young men, who live at the foot of the mountains. The taste for a wandering and vagabond life, the idea of a certain independence amidst forests, leads them to prefer this employment to the sedentary and monotonous labor of cities.[28]

The description is striking not only because of Humboldt's anxiety at seeing optically white men like himself doing something so degrading as carrying another human being on their backs. The description is compelling also because Humboldt's analysis of the motivations of the "young men" so resemble his own. The only way in which he can explain the pain they suffer and the dangers they face in their travels is by projecting onto them his own desires, his *wanderlust*, his need to escape the sedentary life that he so feared. Paradoxically, a still-young Humboldt sees his past beauty, strength, and youth in the *carguero*. But the *carguero* represents more than Humboldt's past; he also stands for Humboldt's desire for future adventure, for a virginal nature awaiting to be explored and mapped. From this perspective, the plate represents the traveler, Humboldt, looking at his own idealized past and future.

Degeneration and the Resisting Other

Humboldt's identification with the *carguero* resulted not only from his youthful fantasies, but also from his Christian charity, and from the scientific form that religious discourse began to take around the middle of the eighteenth century. He identified with the *carguero* partly because of his anxieties about degeneration, a dystopia that became very popular by the end of the nineteenth century.

Probably the most famous French traveler and naturalist of the eighteenth century, George-Louis Leclerc de Buffon (1707–1788), believed that members of a species could breed with each other, but not with representatives of any other species. He gave scientific form to the religious maxim "like begets like," and suggested that all human races originated in a single human species, but had deviated from the primitive type. Such distinctions between racial deviation and racial difference were the core of the arguments of monogenists and later degenerationists concerned with the decline of the "European race."

Following Buffon, Humboldt also argued for the principle of a single race maintaining "the unity of the human species."[29] Anticipating the discourse on degeneracy, he further argued that environment was responsible for racial deviations. But, uneasy about the biological continuity he so famously assumed between the Americans and the Europeans, he also stressed the uniqueness of the American races. As we have seen, he argued that Americans were not only a deviation but also an anomaly. They should have been extinct, he claimed, and were preserved only by isolation, distance, and climate.[30]

We find this move from easy closeness to uneasy distance repeated in Humboldt's description of the American landscape, and in particular in his famous description of the Tequendama Falls. In keeping with his cosmological perspective, he tells the story of the creation of the falls to illustrate the similarities between the myths of the people who had inhabited the plateau of Bogotá and the religious traditions of several nations of the old continent.[31] The description ends, however, with a view of the Tequendama from below. Abandoning his lofty perspective and putting his life at risk, Humboldt describes the view after a three-hour-long descent down a ravine, a descent that dramatizes Humboldt's change in perspective. Humboldt's description of the falls begins by placing the narrator on a monumental and ordered temporal plane, but ends with a personal reflection about the end of the narrator's life.

Humboldt's work then articulates domestic anxieties that take more than one form, but that, despite their differences, all inform his temporal and spatial mappings of the Other. In our earlier analysis we moved between

Humboldt's monumental time and his notion of a temporal subject falling from its earlier heights, or between his imperial nostalgic gaze and his eye/I anxious about its future safety. Now the caveats in Humboldt's arguments and the changes in his perspective suggest that the primitive landscapes and the extinct races that he "saw" in America were too close for comfort. They suggest that Humboldt and Europeans like him were carried by the romantic current underlying their scientific discourse, and followed these bodies down in their fall, or in their deviation from racial perfection, anxiously suspecting their own degeneration.

But if Humboldt represents images of the colonial Other determined by such metropolitan issues, his work also stands for the remains of the agency of the Other, as it traces the *carguero*'s response to the traveler's mapping practices. Indeed, Humboldt's subtle modification of the monarchy's hierarchy can also be interpreted as an adjustment to a threat implied in the plate depicting the *carguero*. The reader will remember that the plate shows a *carguero* carrying an empty chair. In so far as that is the case, the European traveler also sees his own absence. In it, he may perhaps see his own violent ejection from the *carguero*'s chair by a figure burdened with the traveler's past and future, and weighted down by the cost of such a burden: the loss of his present Self and future prospects.

Humboldt's complaints throughout his *Personal Narrative* about his "mulatto" guides who hurry him along or delay him are further traces of that erased Other, as are his references to the famous mutiny on the *Bounty*.[32] The reference to Captain William Bligh's miraculous survival presumably illustrates a scientific meditation on the comparison between hunger and cold. But it occurs to him when he is describing a trip up the Manzanares river in a canoe guided by rowers called *bogas*, who are compared to river *cargueros* in many travelogues. It is significant that the reference to Bligh occurs to Humboldt right after he describes the vivid impression left on him by the horrible sight of a sale of slaves, which leaves him unable to concentrate on his meteorological work. Humboldt's description of the violence practiced on the bodies of the slaves gives the reader the context in which to place the image of Bligh set adrift by the mutineers in the *Bounty*: the mutiny is a violent response to a violent repression. The threat of a mutiny similarly haunts the traveling Humboldt, transported by guides of African descent.

Such signs of resistance, willfulness, and violence are erased from the idealized description of the European travelers. But traces of them remain, like Humboldt's anxious reference to the mutiny. They suggest that the Other's view of the future is different from the traveler's idealized and idealizing gaze. Traces like the *carguero*'s empty chair suggest that the *carguero*'s future is not a pretty sight, and will lead at best to delays, and at worst to the violent overthrow of the traveler from his superior position.

These troubling encounters with the Other, combined with Humboldt's transplanted and accumulating fears and anxieties, make inroads into his network of ordering maps. Those inroads turn the grids of his virtual maps into tears. Through these holes or *lacunae* in his work, Humboldt sees his European reality deteriorate. The identification with an idealized monumental past, the simultaneous awareness of an uncertain and even collapsing future, and the effect of the agency of the Other combine to highlight for Humboldt the weakened state of the Holy Roman Empire.

As much is suggested in a letter Humboldt wrote to Frederick William III (king of Prussia since 1797) upon his return from his travels, only two years before the catastrophic battle of Valmy.[33] In a mirror image of Moctezuma's ineffective attempt to postpone his ill-fated future with gifts and excuses, Humboldt postpones his own future with similarly ineffective gifts and telling excuses. On the one hand, Humboldt says that he is eager to return to Berlin to begin preparing his manuscripts and sketches for publication— probably the most sedentary of occupations. On the other hand, he claims that he cannot do so because northern Germany's cold winter would destroy his health, now used to warmer climates. He adds that during his absence he has lost his family, and his remaining brother awaits him in southern Italy. The ordering map and its opposite sets of coordinates is familiar to the reader: north and south, high and low, cold and hot. But as Humboldt turns his mapping practices toward Europe, the meanings attached to the coordinates have changed. A cold climate, a high elevation, and a northerly location are now the coordinates for illness. Moreover, the family marked by its dying members and the Fatherland made distinct by its dangerous coordinates form an ominous temporal landscape: Humboldt's inescapable future. But they also combine into a future trip that Humboldt postpones—a postponement that suggests the world that Humboldt sees through the tears on his virtual maps is dissolving. It reminds the reader of the *carguero*'s delay tactics, and it suggests that Humboldt has followed in the *carguero*'s tracks to a critical perspective on his own country. In the end, threatened by Europe, Humboldt identifies with a futureless and homeless Other.

Mollien's Notion of Time and Degeneration

Mary Louise Pratt has convincingly shown that a "capitalist vanguard" followed Humboldt's expedition to America. During the first three decades of the nineteenth century, European travelers, mostly from England and France, visited Central and South America, and were responsible for a "narrative of success."[34] Pratt describes it as a "goal-oriented" narrative of sustained progress and heroic achievement. The travel accounts presented a confident sense of self, and an optimism about the future of the European subject. They also projected on to the landscape a "negative aesthetic" of backwardness and neglect that legitimated European interventionism.[35] Pratt further argues that liberal, urban, Spanish Americans shared the aspirations of this capitalist vanguard, but "did not adopt their discourse wholesale as their own."[36] She concludes that, instead, South America's educated elites turned "to the utopian American esthetic codified by Humboldt."[37]

Pratt is right to point out the turn back to Humboldt signified by liberal projects such as the Chorography Commission. And yet, a close examination of the travel account of one of these economic adventurers also suggests that not all of the travel narratives produced by the "capitalist vanguard" were optimistic. Indeed, it suggests that the vanguard's critical concept of time and race laid the groundwork for the changes in the mapping and signifying practices of the South American liberal elites.

Gaspard Théodore Mollien was a European soldier *cum* merchant. Like Humboldt, he was concerned with degeneration at home and abroad, and he associated it with heredity. Unlike Humboldt, however, Mollien emphasized biology over environment. In *Travels in the Republic of Colombia in the Year of* 1823,[38] he argued that miscegenation between the so-called black, the indian, and the European "races" deviated the body from its primitive type, and "weakened its constitution."[39] Such notions, however, represented not a rejection of but an adjustment to Humboldt's comparable network of time, race, and space. Despite Mollien's unpopular reception by Spanish American readers, the adjustment would prove significant to their critical perspective on themselves, and on their country as a bodyscape and a landscape in a sustained state of crisis. If the lettered elites returned to Humboldt, as Pratt astutely claims, here I will argue that they did so only through the concept of crisis elaborated by members of the "capitalist vanguard" like Mollien.

For Mollien, New Granada's "white" population had two apparently contradictory temporal problems. Not only was it intellectually backward, but it was also "precociously decrepit."[40] The problems were due in part to the endemic nature of "incurable" diseases such as goiter (*bocio* or *coto* in Spanish).[41] According to an anxiety-ridden Mollien, the endemic disease preferred the "Euroamerican race," sending the "Creole minds" back to the past while propelling their bodies forward to an early death. The temporal anxiety that frames the description of this disease, and its European-like subject, suggest that Mollien's complementary fantasies of a future world overcome by a primitive "black race" in fact displaced a concern with the degeneration of the "European race."[42]

Likewise, Mollien's description of the American landscape foregrounded his anxieties about miscegenation, or the uncontrolled movement and mixing of different bloods and races. Unlike Humboldt, Mollien does not mention Muisca mythology in his description of the Tequendama Falls. Instead he relates two significant anecdotes. He tells the story of Simón Bolívar (the hero of the wars of independence from Spain) boldly jumping up on the rocks overlooking the falls to fathom them, as if "desiring to grow impassive, to get used to gauging the abyss of revolutions by facing those of nature."[43] He then tells the equally striking story of a Spanish viceroy of Bogotá who, defeated by Bolívar, decided to leave his mark by throwing living bulls down the falls, just to see their "broken members bloodying the rocks" at the bottom of the Tequendama. The stories offer insights into the Spanish-American revolution. They suggest that the wars of independence will result in a felicitous transition of power from a perverse and cowardly Spanish viceroy to a brave Bolívar.

But the same stories also offer a different insight into the outcome of the ongoing revolution. Both stories compare the end of revolution to a violent fall over which these two opposite figures are presiding. Bolívar and the viceroy are repeating, if changing, images. They are overseeing a common descent marked by the uncontrolled loss of blood. The viceroy's perverse entertainment gains particular significance in Mollien's text, which is so concerned with miscegenation that it attributes the defeat of the Spanish troops to a constitutional weakness resulting from years of racial mixture. For Mollien, the Tequendama is a dangerous site that combines time and race, which he is quick to leave. Unlike Humboldt before him, it is a site into which Mollien dares not descend. If Humboldt felt his own mortality in such sites, Mollien envisioned there the degeneration of the "European race."

Local anxieties determined not only what the travelers "felt" and "saw," but also the interpretation of their texts and illustrations by other Europeans. Such interpretations were not limited to travel narratives: Europeans shipped to Paris samples of the curiosities they found in their travels abroad, including human beings, living examples of the "extinct" human races encountered. Upon arrival in Europe, however, these "examples" lost their uniqueness. Thus, Benedict Morel—famous for turning degeneration into a clinical event in 1857—remarked that a photographic plate of a twenty-two-year-old French woman suffering from incurable cretinism reminded him of "ancient Mexicans" exhibited in Paris (fig. 2).[44]

Cretinism, called "a major medical puzzle" of the thirties and forties by one historian of medicine, was described by Honoré de Balzac in *The Country Doctor* in 1833 as a moral and physical disease affecting the body and mind of the French peasant.[45] Like degeneration, the form of cretinism was temporal. It was marked, on the one hand, by the arrest of the biological clock as the development of reproductive organs ceased. On the other hand, it was also distinguished by a regression of intellectual capacities ending in stupidity or imbecility. Thus, like goiter, cretinism threatened Europeans with atavism or with early senility. It is not surprising, then, that when Europeans traveled to America, they "saw" and were preoccupied by a state of widespread illness

Fig. 2. "Adelaide . . . 22 years old. Microcephalic. General Cessation of Development." In Benedict Morel, *Trait des dégénerescences* (New York: Arno Press, 1976), appendix, plate 2. Copied with permission from Ayer Company Publishers, Inc., North Stratford, NH 03590.

2. Adélaïde . . . 22 ans. Microcéphalic.
Arrêt général de développement.

among the population physically most like their own, whose temporal symptoms were equivalent to those suffered by cretins, and later by degenerates.

The distinct temporal nature of goiter, cretinism, and degeneration also relates these diseases to the legacy of the continuing revolutionary process in Europe. The degenerate that Mollien "saw" in America was slightly different from the deviated and extinct races that Humboldt "saw." For Mollien, degeneration was the legacy of a change in the sense of time and history in Europe. This change resulted partly from the meteoric rise and fall of both the revolutionary regime and the Napoleonic empire, as well as from the improbable restoration of the French monarchy. Perhaps these cycles, revisited between 1830 and 1852, were responsible for a sense of temporal repetition and historical parody best expressed later in the century by Karl Marx and Friederich Nietzsche. There is no question, however, that their temporal schemes included a pathological dimension apparently substantiated by the travels of Europeans through their own provincial states.[46]

Patrician Optimism

Probably influenced by the optimistic thrust of the "capitalist vanguard" as described by Pratt, many of the American patricians who organized the governments that emerged after the revolutionary wars "saw" relatively easy solutions to these temporal, spatial, and racial problems. Some even argued that the problems diagnosed by the European travelers could be used to the Americans' advantage. At the end of his travel account in 1823, and expressing surprise at their unbounded optimism, Mollien records that Colombians felt that even the nation's "insalubrious coastal climate" worked in their favor.[47] Members of the liberal elite told a skeptical Mollien that disease acted like a protective cordon or barrier preventing a European invasion. They conjured for Mollien his own (and still pervasive) notion of "race" as a biological and hereditary feature susceptible to certain diseases. Following Mollien's understanding of the degenerate individual whose "pathological proclivities would worsen under the influence of a noxious environment," lettered members of the privileged social classes threatened Europeans with their own feared degeneration.[48]

When applying the same concept to themselves, however, they changed its ideological charge. They suggested that longstanding acclimatization had the opposite effect on their own constitution, making their hybrid race more resistant to the diseases of the torrid zone. Only years of life in the tropics, they suggested, fine-tuned the "European race" to the American environment. Wielding what Melbourne Tapper has called a "racial formalism" that would determine the discourse on health and race by the end of the century, liberal elites thus legitimated their authority and authorized their self-government.

Patrician liberals further manipulated the racialistic scientific theories of their European counterparts to argue that the effectiveness of climate as a protective barrier depended on finding a solution to a racial problem distinct from, but related to, degeneration.[49] Drawing from the medical theories of European naturalists like Jean Baptiste Boussingault (1802–1887) and Humboldt, and from travel accounts like Mollien's, they suggested that different races in their so-called "pure state" exhibited unequal physical resistance to environmental influences. From this perspective, the "white European race" was perceived to be at one end of a continuum of immunity that had the pure "black" and "indian races" at its opposite pole.[50] To be effective, and lasting, the government could not be in the delicate hands of a purely "European race." Conversely, a purely "black" or "indian" race represented a powerful challenge to a hybrid "creole race," which was imagined occupying the middle ground of the same continuum. Such a formidable challenge, many patricians began to suspect, would not permit as violent an institution as slavery to remain unreformed. Not surprisingly, Mollien reported in his travel account that the answer preferred by the patricians to the threat of a stronger race was different from his own. It seemed unreasonable to Mollien, but not to us, that many *letrados* would not reinforce the institution of slavery as a means to keeping political control. "The new government," Mollien complains, "has shown itself very favorable to the slaves, and thanks to a law passed only recently, in forty years there will be none remaining in the republic."[51] Instead, he reports, they tend to substitute the "black" work force with the steam engine, while replacing visually different bodies with Europeans through an active policy of immigration.[52] Though this solution may strike the modern reader as the *letrado*'s manipulation of European racialistic theories, it could not but surprise Mollien.

Such selective processes and their optimistic prognoses survived well into the fourth decade of the nineteenth century, as suggested by foundational texts like *Facundo, Civilization and Barbarism*, published in 1845.[53] They were grandiose attempts to find less violent solutions to the racial conflict that slavery had sustained and intensified.[54] As has been argued before, such ambitious solutions tried to incorporate the unruly romantic passions with an enlightened project of law and order. Similarly, these solutions displaced "some of the contradictions involved in trying to legitimate hierarchical societies through egalitarian ideologies."[55] They originated in the fantastic promise of the European and American revolutions: the appearance of a bright future emerging *ex nihilo*, as a founding temporal rupture.[56]

The members of the Chorography Commission wrote after this initial wave of optimism had passed. They had to confront both a belated abolition of slavery and a continuing political instability. It is not surprising, then, that they were skeptical about the panaceas imagined by their patrician elders. They became skeptical about the benefits of abolition, and believed that the chains of slavery extended well beyond the apparent disappearance of the institution. For one thing, the younger *letrados* considered that the effects of slavery were long-lasting, and that they were the cause of continuing social and political stasis. Drawing from European discussions about the causal relationship between slavery and degeneration, Colombian writers like Manuel Ancízar, Santiago Pérez, and Manuel Pombo imagined these figurative chains as a force pulling the American body back from its future, as well as back to the past. Similarly, futuristic-sounding efforts to civilize turned into symptoms of degeneration's temporal crisis. As the Magdalena river became littered with sunken steamships, the young *letrados* criticized the earlier vision of a civilizing process dependent on technological advances like the steam engine. Such easy solutions came to be seen as further obstacles to progress.

Incorporating Temporal Anxieties

If Humboldt's morphing textual empire idealized the past as well as the future, if it projected different and changing maps onto a landscape in disarray, the Chorography Commission set out to reorganize and remap time and space further. The patrician *letrados* who studied Humboldt's maps, Boussingault's medical papers, and Mollien's travel narratives developed their own landscapes and bodyscapes, fixing time, space, and race according to their own needs. From Humboldt they learned to seek an idealized order within the apparent chaos. From Mollien, they interiorized a balanced but less than ideal sense of their own racial hybridity. Following in Humboldt's and Mollien's footsteps, the younger and more pragmatic *letrados* of the commission set out to give structure to a chaos they perceived as being normative.

The members of the Chorography Commission saw the past of the colonies as chaotic. Colombia's past not only involved oriental-like fables and myths, it also included the Spanish conquest (with its accompanying violent legend), the legacy of the institution of slavery (abolished during the second year of the commission's work, 1851), the wars of independence, and the numerous and costly civil wars occurring roughly once every ten years between 1830 and 1860.

Moreover, temporal coordinates like the past, the present, and the future lost their uniqueness to a more dynamic temporal organization based on repetition and change. Informed by experiences, desires, and anxieties both similar to and different from those expressed by Humboldt, the members of the Chorography Commission had a different notion of time. Time for them was neither cosmic nor a series of unique moments within an economy of temporal scarcity. The present was not a unique upheaval similar to the revolution that threatened Humboldt's imperial gaze, insinuated by the *carguero*'s empty chair. Instead, time became for them what Daniel Pick has suggestively described as "the experience of the pathological reproduction and transformation of revolution."[57] Chorographic time, as it were, paradoxically blended together repetition and change. Time became an endless repetition of critical moments, even as all moments of crisis were unique and irreducible to previous models. Put yet another way, the country was described as experiencing a degenerative condition, whose specific symptoms were dynamic and transformational, but were always dangerous and retrogressive.

Similarly, the idea of ordering space by "fixing" its coordinates gradually gave way to that of disciplining by preserving flow or movement between spaces that now appeared to be "too closed," and were in need of "opening up." Indeed, like the members of the "capitalist vanguard," Codazzi and his fellow travelers viewed themselves as demystifying for their readers the state of the national landscape, repeating and adjusting Humboldt's common-places. The geological catastrophes that Humboldt had placed in the distant past and had compared to the ancient geological history of the old continent appeared differently to the American chorographers. Using the writings of Humboldt himself as evidence, *letrados* like Ancízar argued not only for the comparative geological youth of the Americas, but also stressed the ever changing shape of its landscape, while contemporaries of Ancízar like Pombo fantasized about its eventual collapse.[58] Indeed, they argued that the ordered classifications and the miniature systems used by the "thinkers from across the oceans" were not applicable to the American landscape.[59]

Pérez's narratives were similarly critical of the idealizing and idealized gaze of lofty travelers like Humboldt, and offered an alternative view of the American landscape. Pérez accompanied Codazzi before and after the Conservative coup d'etat in 1854, which, among other things, showed the precariousness of the geographic order liberals had imposed with the Constitution of 1853. After the coup, the push to provincial autonomy was moderated by a reduction in the number of provinces as well as by the abolition of the canton (previously the smallest geographical unit used to divide the territory). In fact, geographic divisions continued to change throughout the tenure of the Chorography Commission, having direct consequences on the maps, descriptions, and tables it produced.[60] In 1857 the twenty-four provinces combined into eight states, forcing Codazzi to redo many of his maps. All told, the republic changed names and constitutions five times between 1832 and 1886, reflecting its mutating political and geographic landscape. It is thus no surprise that Ancízar and Pérez turned Humboldt's bodyscapes and landscapes into allegories of political and geographic disorder.[61]

In further contrast to Humboldt's cosmological perspective, and different as well from the global commercial agenda of the "capitalist vanguard," the Chorography Commission was provincial by mandate. If Humboldt's aerial perspective was meant to provide widespread information to expanding commercial empires, and the modified perspective of the English and French entrepreneurs continued to serve a similar agenda, the Chorography Commission's provincial perspective was intended to help the emerging colonial administration enforce the law. Its commission was clearly laid out by the secretary of exterior relations of 1852 in a letter published in Codazzi's *Physical Geography*. In that letter, the secretary states that in a time of increasing decentralization, and in order to maintain a general state of order, it becomes necessary to delineate better the geographic and governmental structure of the provinces.[62] In accordance with this mandate, Codazzi divided *Physical Geography* into chapters describing and fixing the boundaries of the provinces of New Granada. As soon as each chapter was finished, Codazzi sent it to the local authorities to improve their governing practices. Already outdated by the time they were published as a whole, the individual chapters of *Physical Geography* had already served their political purpose. They were divided into sections describing the cantons of each province, accompanied by synoptic tables detailing the distances between every town, their distance from sea level, their climate, their riches, and the number of men fit for military duty—revealing the strategic function of the commission as a means to bring order to the republic's political disarray. Such knowledge would come in handy in 1854 when Codazzi was appointed chief of staff of the Northern Army, charged with containing the rebellious forces of General José María Melo. Given this particular kind of strategic knowledge, recorded for immediate use, it is no surprise that despite the idealistic intentions of the liberal government that commissioned the reports, the combined results of Codazzi's expedition never resulted in a multivolume work.

Despite these important differences, the commission's provincial perspective and policing function incorporated Humboldt's temporal anxieties. Indeed, its texts, maps, and illustrations owed much to Humboldt's representation of an uncertain future, a future threatening disorder and difference, and of a temporal economy based on the concept of future scarcity and loss, best expressed by Humboldt's comments about his mortality.

A plate meant to accompany Pérez's portrait of the *carguero*, entitled "The Way to Nóvita in the Mountains of Tamaná," shows the composite figure of the *carguero* moving through space; it is also an allegory of temporal anxieties (fig. 3). On the one hand the watercolor, like Pérez's account, represents a precarious political balancing act. Pérez's contrast between the serious and self-absorbed lofty traveler and the joking *carguero* is here slightly modified to show the traveler's necessary concentration in his reading, which makes him oblivious to the danger that lies immediately under him, and makes the *carguero* smile and tread with confidence despite the danger of falling and the dangerous waterfall. What in Pérez's account is a meaningful conflict designed to underscore the tensions between eternal mapping practices and actual critical moments is here represented as a negotiated solution: conjuring the figure of a trapeze artist, the traveler balances on the *carguero*'s back, as the *carguero* balances on the log.

But most significantly, the watercolor also shows a *temporal* balancing act. The path just traversed is almost invisible and barely glimpsed by both the absorbed reader inside the illustration and by the viewer outside the watercolor. What lies ahead is likewise only hinted at by the invisibility of the bridge's landing and by the bend in the road, corner right. Time is further suggested by the stream and waterfall whose origins are just as invisible as their end. Anxiety over an uncertain future, a sense of threatening disorder, and an impending sensation of loss are all part of the watercolor, but unlike

Fig. 3. *Chocó: The Way to Novita in the Mountain of Tamaná, 1853.* By N. N. In Jaime Ardila and Camilo Lleras, *Batalla contra el olvido* (Bogotá: OP Gráficas, 1985), 181, plate 94.

in Humboldt's illustration, here they are front and center. Indeed, the subject of this painting is the response to a critical moment in time: the fear surrounding the *carguero*'s very next step.

The moment is critical and its outcome may be uncertain, but the crisis is certainly not unique. Pérez highlighted the repetition in time of the same moment of crisis in his description of the *carguero*. Having survived the obstacle on the road, the traveler looks back at the broad tree trunk that hit him and conjures the image of numerous past and future travelers paying the same toll of passage: an eternal repetition of critical moments whose outcome is indeterminate.[63] The present, then, is not a unique upheaval but a familiar moment of crisis, even if its outcome is uncertain.

In his references to the territory's decadence, Codazzi repeats Pérez's sense of familiarity with the state of crisis, blending Humboldt's anxiety about the future with Mollien's concern about degeneration.

It has been thirty-two years since I last travelled through these parts in an important military commission and I can assure you that, if today I have seen an increase in the African population that inhabits riverbanks that were once almost deserted, I have also noticed the regression of these people. Nóvita is not what it used to be in 1820 and Quibdó is almost in the same state I found it back then, with the difference that in the latter city there have been two or three fires that have set her back, while Nóvita owes its decadence to the exodus or death of a number of industrious men that once dedicated themselves to the exploitation in great scale of the magnificent mineral.[64]

Like Mollien, Codazzi was also a soldier *cum* merchant interested in advancing his military career and increasing his wealth. He also came to wage war against the Spanish metropolis during the wars of independence, and to profit from the hitherto closed markets of the Spanish colonies. Codazzi's remark was clearly meant to conjure for the governor of the province of Chocó that military past, and to suggest that the crisis the wars tried to resolve had now returned in a different form. Time may have passed since the wars of independence, Codazzi suggests, but the critical state of Nóvita and Quibdó has not changed. Instead, he fears that it may have worsened, as the towns have decayed and regressed while the number of Africans has increased.

Intersecting time and race, Codazzi revisited Mollien's discursive site for degeneration, the disease that by the end of the century would become the "condition of conditions, the ultimate signifier of pathology,"[65] and, I would add, of crisis. Mollien and Codazzi were not alone in demarcating this discoursive site associating time with space and race. Both Pérez and Ancízar linked time and race to the body of the people inhabiting the plateaux, whom they "saw" as bearing the stigmata of the disease.[66]

Adjusting the Distance from the Other

Thus, the rejection of patrician optimism implied that the nature of the problem had not changed since Mollien, that it was just as pressing for the members of the Chorography Commission. Indeed, Mollien's site of racial and temporal crisis was successfully interiorized and developed even by the European head of the commission. A composite picture of this degenerate site emerges when Codazzi's early memoirs of his campaign during the wars of independence are compared with the later texts written during the chorography expedition.

In his 1825 account, Codazzi does not associate the loss of blood with the wars against the Spaniards. Instead, he focuses on a parallel war against nature, whose blood-sucking insects and vampires multiply in sites that are always close to bodies of water.[67] Codazzi further emphasizes the link between environment and loss of blood when he compares the "diabolical" effect of the American landscape to losing the body's extremities to gangrene.[68] Codazzi's early focus on blood loss and his references to the fragmented "European body" were strategies familiar to European travel accounts, similar in their attempts to distance themselves from a disease that was already interiorized.

In his later work, however, Codazzi challenged the accompanying claim to intellectual superiority that balanced this fear of degeneration. He argued that the "vain European race," claiming "supposed natural privileges," would be morally and intellectually humiliated if it found itself under circumstances similar to those of the "barbarous indian."[69] Moreover, Codazzi substituted his early metaphor of a foreign body losing its blood and its members with a national body whose members were suffering from tumors caused by lack of proper circulation in the blood.[70]

By the time Codazzi started working for the Chorography Commission, he had lived in Venezuela for twenty-three years, was married to the daughter of a royalist governor, and had a family of eight children living in Bogotá. Perhaps these changes explain his focus on internal rather than external threats, as well as his concentration on blood circulation rather than on blood loss. These changes in his personal life, combined with his commission to map the provinces of New Granada, certainly explain his switching emphasis from the threat to a "European body" to the degeneration of a national body.

Despite his differences with Humboldt and Mollien, Codazzi's description of New Granada was a modification, not a rejection, of their asymptotal relationship with the American Other. While Codazzi's descriptions of the degenerate site reflected a reduction in the distance between the European Self and the American Other, the difference was still maintained through a clinical discourse whose grammatical "cues" placed the Other in the role of the patient, and Codazzi in the role of the examining doctor.

The site of degeneration was similarly developed by Henry Price, in his 1852 watercolor of Guadalupe Falls (fig. 4). A comparison between Price's picture of the falls, and Humboldt's plate of the Tequendama reveals a number of interesting differences. Humboldt's plate, perhaps an ordering response to his anxious descent, evokes in the viewer a sense of frozen time and a monumental perspective (fig. 5). The small and anonymous human figures on top of the Tequendama are a visual coordinate establishing the size of the falls and the length of the drop. They also suggest the relative safety of the visitors, even though they are standing on a rock 175 meters high. The detail with which the water is painted going downward and splashing upward stops the motion of the water in an eternal moment. If the viewer has some sense of the water's violence as it falls that great distance, it is a sense of controlled violence. The water is constrained by the perspective of the artist, who does not sketch the waterfall from its front, which would flatten out the bordering precipice. Instead, he takes a one-quarter perspective, which emphasizes the rocky margin and accentuates its monumental constraint with chiaroscuro.

In contrast to the soothing and distancing strategies of that plate, Price's darker watercolor brings the viewer in and provokes anxiety and fear. First, he places Codazzi in the bottom right corner, looking out and establishing a visual link with the viewer. Price's placement of the figure of Codazzi at the bottom of the falls not only brings the viewer in, but also amplifies the degenerate site self-consciously to include not only the American Other, but also the European Self. It calls into question Codazzi's grammatical distance. Second, his technique, or the speed with which Price sketches the waterfall, results in a lack of surrounding detail, focusing the observer's attention on the water's swift downward movement. Finally, his frontal perspective flattens out the sides of the waterfall, emphasizing the uncontrolled violence of the water, which, significantly, hits several obstacles along the way and seems to explode right out of its banks.

Ancízar's work was informed by a similar repetition and amplification of the degenerate site.[71] He too was concerned about a nation steadily headed toward depopulation, and about the speed of its degeneration. Unlike Codazzi, however, Ancízar develops the site of degeneration while grammatically implicating himself in it. Following Humboldt's and Codazzi's descent down the dangerous falls, Ancízar begins *Alpha's Pilgrimage*[72] with an ominous image of a waterfall, and ends it with the closing image of a whirlpool dragging down a collective "we."

Ancízar is, in turn, an appropriate predecessor to Pérez's description of the Chocó as a river fragmented (*quebrado*) by its numerous anonymous and

Fig. 4. *Medellin: Guadalupe Falls, 1852.* By Henri Price. In Jaime Ardila and Camilo Lleras, *Batalla contra el olvido* (Bogotá: OP Gráficas, 1985), 165, plate 75.

Fig. 5. *Tequendama Falls.* Drawn from a sketch by Humboldt. Engraved by Gueline in Rome. In Alexander Humboldt, *Atlas pittoresque du voyage: Vues des Cordillères, et monumens des peuples indigènes de l'Amérique* (Amsterdam: Theatrum Orbus Terrarum Ltd.; and New York: Plenum Publishing Corporation, 1971–1972), vol. 7, plate 6. The Hague, Koninklijke Biblitheek.

atemporal streams, which, if they blend, mix into one confused and confusing mass.

> Forever, along both riverbanks, stretch intricate and thick jungles, where the vegetation is barely contained, and through which run, uncharted, without a name and without a history, a multitude of differently sized streams, that come to an end when they join in the current where they all become jumbled.[73]

Pérez's description of a river eternally fed by uncharted and different streams that are themselves outside time suggests the transformation of Humboldt's earlier concern with temporal scarcity into a normative sense of temporal repetition and change, marked by the image of a river eternally fed by disordered strands of disconnected time. As such, it repeats Codazzi's metaphor of the body politic as an organism whose blood is not lost but runs outside its proper banks, leading to serious racial problems. Pérez projects Codazzi's organic metaphors onto bodyscapes like the figure of the *carguero*, a forward-moving figure in "reflective backwardness". But Pérez also saw the problem differently from Codazzi. Like Ancízar, he assigns a grammatical "we" to the composite figure.[74] The chorographers' increasing attention to their kinship with the object of analysis points to their concern with modes of self-government and self-definition: perhaps the two principal results of the Chorography Commission.

Military Roads and Parallel Times

The repeated return of the crisis in different forms suggested to the Chorography Commission that a new approach to regeneration was needed: the cure should be different from the solutions first proposed by the patrician elders; it should not be quick and violent; it should not be imposed from the outside; it should be better adjusted to the form of the disease. As such, the cure's constitutive elements became versatility and speed, and its watchwords became movement and progress. Following Codazzi, the Chorography Commission changed the streams crisscrossing the country into metaphorical blood vessels running through a living organism. Its main recommendation was the construction of better channels of communication to facilitate, and also to regulate, the movement of different bloods through an unruly landscape that stood for a normatively diseased body.[75] In other words, the commission called for provincial roads, a less traumatic and more practical intervention than isolating and controlling "contaminated bodies" in order to replace them with "healthy" European specimens.

Provincial roads, or better still, military roads (*carreteras militares*), appeared side by side with police in the texts of the commission.[76] Indeed, police or *policía*, both as a set of laws and as the group of people charged with enforcing them, is a key concept to understand the function of the roads imagined and laid out by the Chorography Commission. Roads were believed necessary to restore order and direction to a population of recently freed slaves, whose slothfulness and idleness were now "seen" as the result of natural accident, and not as the fallout of biology and heredity as Mollien and the patrician *letrados* had suggested.[77] Provincial roads were the imagined solution to the slave's dangerous, newly gained independence.[78]

But provincial roads also suggested the ideal of self-administration, as money, resources, and commerce flowed directly into local, not foreign, hands. Roads represented a self-policing ideal appropriate not only to a more federalist type of government, but also to a change in the liberal political climate that had finally enforced the abolition of slavery. The new concern for the political rights of "blacks" refocused the attention away from violent means of control to personal responsibility. A focus on duty and morality became the point of intervention of an emerging government grappling with the notion of human rights.[79] "Blacks," Codazzi argued, could and should police themselves.[80] Provincial roads were a fitting means to this end, playing an important role in turning "unruly blacks and indians" into citizens, teaching them how to practice discipline on themselves.

If the long road to the internal moral and physical regeneration of the provinces called for a different sense of space and order, autonomous from the central liberal administration, it also called for a sense of time better adjusted to the nature of the problem. Clearly, more time was needed: lengthy exposure to a supposedly contaminating environment had lodged degeneration deep in the American constitution, and it would be a long time before regeneration.[81] This led Codazzi to extend the deadline for finding an effective cure, which postponed the nation's destiny and allayed the fears of its citizens.

Oblivious to the catastrophic predictions of doomsayers, the commission instead emphasized practical movement within a parallel time frame, what Benedict Anderson has aptly called "a complex gloss on the word meanwhile."[82] If the river of time flowed inexorably downstream, the multiplying textual and material works of the commission made digressions that would delay the impending end of the metaphorical river. Like the national streams in Pérez's image, the commission was consciously ahistorical. Its end was postponed over and over again, even as it produced texts and maps that became obsolete soon after they were written. The government complained, withholding funds, but Codazzi did not stop. He kept going "without rest and without haste,"[83] focusing on constant movement, and oblivious to deadlines. The government was forced to go along, recalcitrant, until Codazzi's death. It was as if the Colombian nation's regeneration had become contingent on the extension of the tenure of the Chorography Commission, on the sustained dissemination of its eternally actualized reports.

Autonomous spaces and parallel times called for self-sacrifice, and Codazzi paid dearly with his own life—he died of malaria during his ninth expedition. Ironically, the commission's strategy for national order similarly called for creoles or *blancos* to leave the scene as soon as the road, or the law, was laid down. (By the end of the century, many of them would escape the provinces altogether, and would set off to wander through Europe instead.) In the new order, "whites" could wander the provinces, but only as impartial and invisible observers. They knew that making room for an autonomous space, and setting in motion a parallel time would inevitably lead to mistakes (*yerros*); they believed, however, that regeneration would come only after such mistakes, after wandering off course (*errando*). *Letrados* feared that regeneration would never come through impatient, direct, and violent agency.[84]

This wandering strategy highlighted the need of an invisibility over which "whites" had, in fact, little control. In Pérez's description of the *carguero* he emphasized the traveler's invisibility by pointing to the *carguero*'s indifference to the traveler. Not only does the *carguero* erase his individuality with the suggestive epithet "white," but he also blissfully ignores the traveler's impassioned reprimand, and holds him instead to an uncomfortable law of immobility. As we have seen, concerns over such disregard run through the travel narratives of Humboldt and Mollien. Pérez's description, however, sets him apart from the heroic stance of the "capitalist vanguard" because it does not represent the traveler as a hero when faced with similar dismissals.[85] Neither does it occupy the lofty perspective of Humboldt, who wishes for an idealized realm of racial harmony. Pérez instead suggests that the *carguero*'s joking dismissal of the traveler is the appropriate response to the situation, a necessary allowance for the traveler's own good. Another *letrado* traveler (David Guarín) put it succinctly when he wrote: "In the end I came to realize that not only nobody noticed me, but that I was even a threat to myself."[86]

Pérez's reference to the proverbial yoke (the *horca caudina*), however, also conveys the humiliating nature of the concession exacted on the traveler. Thus, his allegory is also critical of the necessary strategies, suggesting that the concessions are also a capitulation, that the traveler has been defeated in his struggle with the *carguero* for authority. In this way, Pérez's allegory, and by extension the works of the Chorography Commission, were critical not only of the lofty immobility of the earlier travelers, but also of the self-sacrifice suggested by the practices of the present ones. Like Humboldt's representation of the empty chair in Perez's allegory, the *letrado*'s frustration was a response both to an interiorized diseased condition and to the agency of a resisting Other.

Conclusion

The informational discourse of Humboldt's works propelled the body of the traveler to an apparently safe perspective and erased the body of the dangerous Other. This double play promised a future profit to empires by domesticating an unruly colonial landscape. Influenced by the practical concerns of the "capitalist vanguard," the provincial discourse of the Chorography Commission instead suggested installing self-governing measures. It also called for moving quickly through the provinces, or removing the body of the "white" traveler from the degenerate site of the Other as soon as possible. It aimed to postpone, rather than imagine away, future disorder.

But if Humboldt's works were riddled with traces of a conflicted relationship between Self and Other, and between competing notions of the Self, the Chorography Commission's works were similarly marked, leading its members to a starker view of the future. The degeneration diagnosed by the commission was both projected outside and perceived to be an integral part of the creole identity of the liberal elites. But the autonomy and self-removal that the commission proposed as a less violent form of management was also resisted by the members of the commission. It was perceived as a capitulation by the elite of the *letrados* when faced with a stronger force resisting control. From Pérez's perspective, the Colombian nation remained stationary, though it appeared to be moving forward. Like the traveler he described, Colombia was perilously walking forward without looking ahead, innocently trusting the steps of a disgruntled *carguero*.

In sum, the sense of Self that emerged from Humboldt's work was an incongruous metropolitan subject whose perception of the Other was mediated by local discourses (historical, political, religious, and naturalist). Moreover, it was a subject who returned to the metropolis with its perspective changed by Humboldt's attempts to map and order the Other. Similarly, the Self that emerged from the mapping practices of the commission was a figure more conscious of the uncertainty of its foundational role than the founding fathers the patrician statesmen imagined themselves to be. It was best described by Ancízar when he compared the Colombian creole to newborn pilgrims of uncertain future, moving like shadows through a legacy of problems and conjectures.[87]

The temporal, spatial, and racial coordinates of this creole subject would prove decisive for the next generation of writers and statesmen, including José María Samper and Jorge Isaacs. Its coordinates were informed not only by Humboldt's travel narratives, but also by those of the "capitalist vanguard." They formed a network determined by Mollien's sense of critical return and Humboldt's sense of radical rupture. The grid described neither the compensatory heroic fictions of the "capitalist vanguard" nor the idealizations of Humboldt. It resulted instead in an inchoate figure, innocently hoping for a future order, and conscious of going back over the steps of earlier travelers: a racially composite fiction that walked back to the future and moved always through the same critical space.

Weaning the Virile Subject

GENDER AND CRISIS IN JOSÉ MARÍA SAMPER AND JORGE ISAACS

The day will come when a great poet, a historian, and a philosopher will write the poem, the history, and the criticism of the entire Colombian revolution, and the most beautiful and instructive pages will be devoted . . . to the women of that absolutely exuberant world.
—José M. Samper, *Ensayo sobre las revoluciones políticas*

María can drag you, and us with you, to a sad misfortune that threatens her. Doctor Mayn is almost certain that she will die young of the same illness that brought down her mother; yesterday she suffered an epileptic fit which will intensify with every attack, and will end in the worst kind of epilepsy.

—Jorge Isaacs, *María*

Introduction

These passages from two very different Colombian texts combine to suggest an identification of the female body with crisis. Such identification is central to the political essay and the novel where it originates. It is also the foundation of a metaphorical network of gendered oppositions cast by these works from different discursive registers. Mind/body, civilization/barbarism, racial purity/defilement, order/chaos, content/form, are just a few of the oppositions engendered in these works, and originating in registers belonging to philosophy, anthropology, ethnology, the physical sciences, and the belles let-tres, respectively.[1] In all of these binary oppositions, the first element is al-ways associated with the male body, the second with the female body. They are deployed to make a collective body both visible and governable, to in-scribe a collective Self with recognizable features that adjust to specific gov-erning practices. The network, however, is also the source of paradoxes that make it impossible to govern that same body.

The first passage comes from a forgotten essay published in 1861 by the writer and politician José María Samper. In that essay, Samper tried to ex-plain the nature of the political and social revolutions that had visited Span-ish America numerous times since the end of the wars of independence and that seemed to him to plague the region. In this passage, Samper points to the abundance and fruitfulness of an "exuberant world" as the cause of the conflicts and revolutions he analyzed. Indeed, Samper here not only makes explicit an equivalence between revolution and nature, but also identifies the bodies of women with revolution, in a move that remains latent in the rest of his essay.

Samper further develops the gender-based opposition with a distinction between instructive substance and beautiful form. He suggests that both the women and the world described in his 350-page "sketch" will be best studied by a learned man working at a more leisurely pace than he—though the reader soon learns that, in fact, Samper's quick writing pace is a blessing in disguise. Samper goes on to point out that these leisurely works will fatally mimic the exuberance of the region's revolutions with their beautiful form, while his more intense sketch "deflowers" or penetrates the most important moments in the political and social history of Spanish America.[2] Samper's in-vestment of his own work with explicitly virile attributes and his warning against a future feminization suggest his need to buttress the gender divide, as well as his anxiety over its structural instability.

One of the men imagined by Samper walked into his life three years later, when a young Jorge Isaacs entered a literary club of which Samper was a prominent member. After hearing Isaacs recite his verses, Samper, along with the other members of *El Mosaico*, signed a letter introducing Isaacs to the reading public as a great poet. Three years after the meeting, Isaacs went on to write the superbly popular novel *María* (1867), a work that in many ways fulfilled Samper's expectations and shared his anxieties.

Following the model imagined by Samper, and hailed as a "beautiful and lyrical" novel by both contemporary critics and present-day readers, *María's* plot revolves around the body of the young woman of the title. The second passage above is from the beginning of the novel, when Efraín and the reader are instructed by Efraín's father about María's hereditary condition. Efraín's father's precautionary statement about María's body is tellingly authorized by the scientific knowledge of another male character (Dr. Mayn), and will result in the symbolically significant separations of Efraín from María and from his mother. Moreover, the passage traces the fatal disease down a maternal line, back to María's mother, Sarah, emphasizing Sarah's blood and her reproductive organs; all of which suggests a identification between crisis and the body of women.

Like Samper's work, *María* is also a meditation on the apparent history of political crises afflicting Colombia in particular and Spanish America in general during the first half of the nineteenth century. In the forty years between Isaacs's birth and the publication of his novel, what is today known as Colombia went through two significant changes in its political configuration—reflected in the changes in its name, from the Great Colombia to the Republic of New Granada (1830), to the United States of Colombia (1863)—four constitutions, four internal military conflicts, and four very different political administrations.

The national dimension of the health crisis diagnosed in the passage is implied by the identification between the body threatening to bring down Efraín's family, and Sarah's biblical namesake, whose barrenness threatened the future of a "mighty nation."[3] Unlike the biblical story, however, Isaacs is concerned not so much with Sarah's barrenness as with her blood's contaminating influence on her people. Isaacs's Sarah is not barren; she has given birth to an equally infirm María. Her illness threatens to be passed on to Efraín's progeny, figuring the threat to the future male citizens of Colombia.

Both passages, then, rely on an implicit metaphor that identifies crisis with woman's reproductive body, and they both delegate its analysis to the mind of male writers. They further suggest that the sexual organs of women's bodies are not simply *an* aspect of the political crisis each author seeks to describe, but its determining aspect. In this chapter I will argue that these authors find the cause of Spanish America's endemic crises in the principle of reproduction itself. For these writers, the reproductive body of women is inherently critical because of two longstanding associations: between the body and death, and between the concept of reproduction and the principles of duality and difference.

It is not surprising, then, that Samper and Isaacs would accompany their representation of women's reproductive bodies as figures for crisis, with anxious references to the Godhead, to Scripture, and to the male figure of the *pater familias*. This combination of references to a binary and gendered opposition suggests that their work is part of a wide constellation of nineteenth-century Western meditations on the deadly threat posed by the body, and by the principle of difference, to the incorporeal, and to its related principle of unity or singularity. For both of these writers, the body of women becomes a symbol for this combined threat. For both of them, separation from that body is the inexorable solution to the crisis that it "naturally" brings about. Separation from the body in general, and from the female reproductive body in particular, however, is not without its problems. Some of the paradoxes that emerge from this dramatic weaning process will be another focus of this chapter.

Difference and Singularity in Degeneration

Samper and Isaacs partake in the ancient configuration of a virile subjectivity.[4] Following the Western philosophical tradition that begins with Plato's *Phaedrus* and *Symposium*, that virile subject depends on the exclusion of, and the separation from, the body. But, as has been noted many times, the repressed body has a way of returning. In *The Republic*, Plato is forced to acknowledge that in spite of their wisdom, those trained to be the leaders of the city will suffer the decay of their race, the result of children "wrongly begat."[5] The body gone awry, associated with reproduction, comes back to haunt the virile subject imagined by Plato in the form of the decay and degeneration of its progeny. More significantly, however, the virile subject that performs this exclusion and separation is paradoxically corporeal, though it depends on a body that deconstructs itself. As Kelly Oliver succinctly puts it: "[it] is the body that represents the overcoming of body. The virile body is the symbol of manliness; manliness is associated with culture; culture is associated with overcoming the body."[6]

Oliver's image of a body overcoming its body conjures Friedrich Nietzsche's discussion of the lessons contained in the paradoxical role of physiological degeneration. Just as degeneration is necessary for evolutionary progress, Nietzsche argues, affirmative life depends on processes of outstripping, overcoming, and reinterpreting.[7] Oliver's and Nietzsche's insights go much farther than Plato's philosophical resignation to a measure of racial degeneration. They go on to expose the nihilism, the loss of origins, the decorporealization that lies at the core of the logic of Western philosophy: the virile body outstripping itself, or degenerating, in order to live. The same logic applies to later versions of this virile subject. Reproduction is both the bane of and the founding principle behind the nineteenth-century clinical form of degeneration.

Since its inception, the theory of degeneration is inextricable from the biblical principle of singularity, both in the guise of the Godhead, and in the form of the singular origin of man. Indeed, in the debates on the origin of man that predate Charles Darwin's 1858 publication of *On the Origin of the Species*, degenerationists (also known as monogenists) held that man originates in a single species, and later degenerates into different races. Positivists contemporary with the debate convincingly argued that the theory of degeneration is "soft on Scripture," because it did not challenge, but in fact seemed to support, the biblical notion of a single Adam.[8] Benedict Morel himself, perhaps the greatest exponent of degeneration theory, suggests the importance of Scripture at the very beginning of his work, when he meditates on the biblical origins of natural law.[9]

Morel's theory of degeneration owes much to the work of the most famous French naturalist of the eighteenth century, who believed that members of a species could breed with each other, but not with representatives of any other species. Before Morel, George-Louis Leclerc de Buffon (1707–1788) argued that all human races originate in a single human species. In fact, he turned the religious maxim of "like begets like" into scientific form. Degenerationists simply take Buffon's theory one step further, concluding that if Buffon is right, then inferior races degenerate from a single species.[10] That is the conclusion reached by Morel in his 1857 *Treaty on Physical, Intellectual and Moral Degenerations of the Human Species and Causes that Produce These Infirm Varieties*, in which he defines degeneration as a "pathological deviation from the normal type of humanity," a definition based on Buffon's ideas about reproduction and on the divine maxim "like begets like."[11]

Degeneration theory, however, is related not only to the divinely inspired principle of identity, but also to its opposite, the principle of difference. This contradictory association can also be traced back to Scripture. Consider the theory's implicit parallel between the Fall from paradise and the degeneration of mankind,[12] a parallel explicitly made in the book of Jeremiah.

> Yet I had planted thee a noble vine, wholly a right seed: how then art thou turned into the degenerate plant of a strange vine unto me?[13]

The prophet Jeremiah, divinely inspired, chastises Israel for abandoning itself to false gods. The chastisement is made in the form of a question that fills the divinity with wonder as it tries to explain to itself man's fallen condition: the great distance that separates the paradisiacal state from man's fallen state. The divinity mourns as it gauges the distance between innocence and guilt, between eternity and temporality, between the divine and the human condition. Yahweh's question suggests wonder and even resentment at the breadth of the gap between man and itself. It asks how could man fall so far as to become unrecognizable to his own maker? How could he become a stranger, an Other to Him? Wasn't man originally made in Yahweh's image?

The divinity's surprise at its difference from degenerate man stresses the Judeo-Christian difference between the spiritual and the material. The divinity suggests that its originally spiritual seed is polluted by the ground in which it grows, displacing the principle of difference away from itself and onto the ground. From this displacement, and from the explicit parallel between degeneration and the Fall of man, emerges the association between degeneration and difference, as well as the definition of the event as the result of a separation between a metaphysically pure and a materially defiled element. This association and this definition pit the event of degeneration against the above principle of singularity, and causes a fundamental tension within degeneration that gives the event its nineteenth-century clinical form.

For Morel, degeneration is a problem of the body, specifically, a problem centered on the reproductive organs of women. Degeneration takes one of two clinical forms: atavism or premature aging. Either normal development is arrested, in which case woman's reproductive functions are never fully developed, or normal development is accelerated, in which case the disease brings about a deterioration in the reproductive system. Both forms lead to a disruption in the female sexual organs; its main symptom is infertility, or barrenness.

Moreover, Morel is best known for his dynamic interpretation of reproduction and heredity, which results in a significant difference between parents and offspring without denying kinship. Following the argument of earlier psychologists, Morel argues that a particular and original trait can be simultaneously transmitted and transformed by the reproductive organs into a similar, not an identical, trait. Thus, Morel ironically turns Buffon's theory of heredity into a theory according to which deviation is the necessary result of reproduction. In other words, "like," according to Morel, begets something both more and less than "like." Reproduction contains for Morel the possibility of radical difference.

If the main symptom of this dynamic principle is infertility, then the consequence of the degenerate's reproduction is clearly its eventual extinction. But if there is no radical difference among the species, what protects mankind from a similar fate, ask Morel's contemporaries? In a footnote to his voluminous tractate, Morel assuages his readers by appealing to a metaphysical intellect. Strictly speaking, he argues, the human species cannot degenerate.[14] Unlike Nietzsche, Morel says that degeneration is opposed to progress, and argues that the mind of God is a stronger influence than the degenerating body of man. Morel asks whether humanity progresses or degenerates, and answers that humanity must progress, since the destiny of mankind is determined by the wisdom of the divinity. Only the belief in a superior, divine intellect prevents him from concluding that degeneration is the destiny of mankind.

Jacques Joseph Moreau (de Tours), in his influential 1859 *Morbid Psychology in Its Relations with the Philosophy of History or of the Influence of Neuroses on Intellectual Dynamics*, agrees with Morel's unwitting suggestion that degeneration is the current destiny of mankind; but like Nietzsche after him, he also disagrees with Morel about the consequences of this endemic condition. Moreau's thesis is that madness is caused by a physiological and pathological condition: a neurotic stimulus (*éréthisme névropathique*). From François-Joseph Victor Broussais (1772–1838) he arrives at his definition of neurosis as irritation of the nerves, or as a physical stimulus to pathological action. Broussais found that physical stimulus of the nerves in the spinal column or in the female sexual organs caused hysteria. Using a parallel model, and applying it to a different gender and organ, Moreau argues that neurosis is a principally male disease that affects the intellect. Like Broussais, Moreau argues that overstimulation leads to physical deterioration and madness:[15] the bigger the brains, the higher the likelihood of error. Unlike Broussais, however, he also argues that pathological irritation can cause intellectual development, even perfection or genius.[16]

Perhaps Moreau's contradictions are proof of this insight. His rigorous materialism brings him back to a virile and transcendental subject.[17] He confirms an *a priori* eternal spirit, even as he attempts to constrain the spirit with physiology. Moreau's version of degeneration reintroduces an eternal subject, albeit in the curious form of pure thought, of pure mind energy. Following the principle of singularity, Moreau traces a connecting line between the reproductive organs of women, the male brain, and the eternal indivisible subject, linking the degenerating body to the metaphysical intellect. Following the principle of difference, however, he imagines the future degenerates as a race of feminized or self-deceived virile subjects.

Morel and Moreau together set the terms of a debate about degeneration that leads to contradictory definitions. On the one hand, they associate it with a principle of difference located in the body's reproductive organs, a principle that leads both Morel and Moreau to see degeneration as the separation of the body from the intellect. On the other hand, they also associate degeneration with a principle of singularity located in a transcendental intellect. This principle leads them to see degeneration as the gradual coming together of mind and body.

In the final analysis, degeneration appears as a displacement of the fear of impending death. Morel and Moreau turn death and decay into a scientific process that can be understood. Regardless of claims to scientific objectivity, however, in their attempt to understand the process of death and decay they must load it with cultural presuppositions. Thus, Morel and Moreau engender the process of degeneration, not only in the sense that they construct it, but also in the sense that they break it down into parts that are associated with two genders. Morel and Moreau make degeneration a tension between two sexed parts of the human being: the mind and the body, the one masculine and the other feminine. According to them degeneration is two contradictory processes at once: It is a process where the degenerate feels the disruptive effects of its feminine element (of its body), and seeks to decorporealize itself, breaking itself up, perpetually overcoming its very nature. It is also a process where the degenerate feels the superior force of a male consciousness and, abandoning itself to the obsessive pursuit of genius, becomes a superior intellect that sadly loses its mind.

Freud's Medusa and Atropos

As Sander Gilman convincingly argues, degeneration was a force to be reckoned with in medical discourse, even by the likes of Sigmund Freud. Gilman makes a strong case for Freud's restructuring of the concept. According to Gilman, Freud (in his letters) substitutes degeneration's dependence on physiologically based theories of heredity with a more "purely psychological explanation."[18] Gilman concludes that Freud's restructuring led to his dismissal of the label as false political rhetoric, moving it out of its sexual context and placing it "where it belongs."[19]

And yet, Gilman admits that this restructuring process did not come easily to Freud, whose early training was very much within a medical tradition imbued with, and shaped by, ethical and moral values. While he questioned the overtly biological model on which degeneration had been based, he did not separate the restructured concept from the realm of childhood illnesses, or from the accompanying Hegelian model of linear historical development or progress. For Freud, degeneration continued to be an inhibition in childhood development, specifically, an obstacle in the child's necessary passage from an egoist to a moralist. Freud significantly translated the child's psychological degeneracy or perversity into an "illness of civilization."[20]

While Gilman does not make much of Freud's implicit association between this inhibition, or illness of civilization, and the female body, he does mention that later in his career Freud uses the restructured concept of degeneration mainly in the context of his discussions on female homosexuality and prostitution. Oliver, on the other hand, explicitly argues that Freud's theory of sexuality is fundamentally indebted to the traditional identification of the female body with nature, and to the complementary identification of the male mind with civilization and culture. Oliver argues that the move from nature to culture is, according to Freud, a necessarily violent move away from an identification with the mother, and a subsequent identification with the father. Following Oliver, the move requires the threat of castration to a subject invested with a male anatomy, and thus inters women in general, and daughters in particular, in what she calls the crypt of nature.[21]

The threat posed by woman's anatomy is perhaps most compellingly theorized by Sigmund Freud in his 1922 commentary on the figure of the Medusa's head. In that essay, Freud argues that the mythological figure describes something without referring directly to it, something horrible that must be simultaneously recognized and denied.[22] The event recognized and denied by the figure of Medusa's head is the metaphorical decapitation of the principle of unity and singularity, castration in Freudian terminology. The sight responsible for this decapitation is the female sexual organ.

Freud had visited this site in his 1914 essay on "The Theme of the Three Caskets," where he analyzes the choice of Portia's prospective husbands in *The Merchant of Venice.* He argues that the suitors' choice among three caskets and King Lear's choice among his three daughters are essentially the same. He writes "[if] we had to do with a dream, it would at once occur to us that caskets are also women, symbols of the essential thing in woman, and therefore of a woman herself, like boxes, large or small, baskets, and so on."[23] Reducing woman to her "essential thing," Freud associates her with the caskets. Most important, however, Freud identifies both caskets and women with death. For Freud, the female sexual and reproductive organ is a synecdoche for the death and ruin associated with the regular order of nature, with natural law.[24] The implacable severity of this law, he continues, is further stamped on the figures of the mythical Moerae (Lachesis, Atropos, and Clotho), who stand for the "three inevitable relations man has with women": the mother, the beloved, and the mother earth.[25]

Thus, while Freud apparently restructures the concept of degeneration in his letters, his theory of sexuality actually develops it further. Freud fleshes out the paradoxical love relationships of the virile subject that emerges out of degeneration theory as a decorporealizing body, or as an insane mind. Freud emphasizes the need to separate violently this virile subject from the crypt of nature, or from the female body where it threatens to remain interred. But, like Hegel before him, Freud makes the threatening female body the very agent of, or the force behind, this separation, placing woman in the paradoxical position of both guardian of nature and origin of culture and civilization.[26] Isaacs's and Samper's attempts to construct a national body out of the same gendered oppositions lead them to similarly contradictory images.

Giving Birth to the Nation

Isaacs's concern with Sarah's body and Efraín's progeny is a form of the preoccupation with reproduction, and with the principle of difference for which reproduction stands. Such anxiety is also at the center of a discourse on degeneration that appears in texts contemporary with *María.* A reference to the story of Sarah, for example, appears in an 1866 publication by the same literary club that had sung Isaacs's praises.[27] In the prologue to the four-volume work, its editors explain the change from the original title, *The Granadians*

Painted by Themselves, to *Museum of Customs and Manners*. They write that the 1861 title was premature, because they were no longer "Granadians" after that date, when the name of the country changed from New Granada to the United States of Colombia. To illustrate the humorous consequences of naming a book before its "birth," the editors go back to the story of Sarah's "ailment." Like Isaacs, they do not focus on Sarah's barrenness, but on her illness. Sarah's illness is the point of departure for a second foundational anecdote of a man who, eager for a male heir, gives an inappropriate name (Washington) to a fetus that turns out to be female. The editors' implicit causal connection between Sarah's infirm body and the birth of a female founder suggests the critical state of a nation whose citizens are weakened by the repeated convulsions of a diseased reproductive national body. In other words, the feminization of the citizen suggests here the ill consequences of the recurring "birth" of their nation, made evident by the unfortunate and temporary changes to the name of their own country. According to the members of El Mosaico, such repeated changes had made Colombians the laughingstock of the Spanish American nations.

Samper's essay similarly contributes to the widespread construction of the metaphor of revolution as the genesis of an "embryonic," "emergent," "incipient," and "new-born" body threatened by its feminine origins and by a subsequent feminizing principle. He identifies three principal moments of crisis in the history of Spanish America (the period before, during, and after its domination by Spain), and he identifies each of these moments with reproduction and with the female body. Before the conquest, he argues, Mother Nature gave birth to an embryonic civilization, to an "infantile mass" that was condemned to economic and political stagnation due to its matrilineal organization.[28] He then explains that, during the conquest, this incipient collective mass was no match for the maturer, though ill-formed progeny of Mother Spain. The colonization that ensued produced another monster, this time an extravagant semibarbaric fetus resulting from the mixture of races.[29] Significantly, Samper emphasized that the newborn was then feminized and degenerated by the equally inept political and economic practices of the Spaniards.[30] Mother Revolution, he suggests, was no more successful than her predecessors. She too produced a monstrous citizen, whose metaphorical macrocephalic body was decapitated during the Spanish attempt at reconquest, pointing to yet another form of metaphorical emasculation.[31]

The principle of difference, in the form of biological reproduction and feminization, is then at the origin of the national crisis as represented by the members of *El Mosaico*. The need to isolate this principle leads Samper to a meditation on race, which in turn leads to the concept of pure difference. Difference takes the form of race in Samper's analysis. But it is not the difference between superior and inferior races that concerns him, it is the problem of racial purity. Racial purity has implications for Samper that go beyond the consequences of countries populated by superior or inferior races. Racial purity creates disquieting social, economic, and political events that transcend the differences between the New and the Old World. A social concern with racial purity, argues Samper, leads to ruptures in the social fabric by creating unnecessary social, economic, and political differences.[32]

Significantly, racial purity, for Samper, is sexually determined. Purity can be confirmed only through the maternal line, he argues.[33] To say pure, for Samper, is mainly to say that the same maternal blood runs through different bodies. In other words, Samper suggests that the European and the natural or primitive New World are organized under the same feminine category of racial purity, and that this category has the paradoxical effect of contaminating the social body. Contamination is, then, the result of the feminine principle of difference in its pure state. It leads to an imbalance in the social body, and creates an indistinct, brutish, feminine body mass, which must be brought back under control.[34]

Cutting the Thread of Life

María's racial purity is a similar disaster waiting to happen. As critics have convincingly argued, *María* is a meditation on the contaminating effect of holding on to racial difference or purity.[35] María's blood is related in the novel to her ethnicity, and is represented as a contaminating influence responsible for her disease, and at least partly responsible for her death. Despite recent, compelling readings of the contradictory role of ethnicity in the novel, the very principle of difference seems more important than the specific origin of María's race. María is not only Jewish; she is so malleable a figure that she is both Jewish and Christian. Moreover, her conversations with Efraín highlight her duplicitous nature; at one point she even schemes with him against the paternal command, thus symbolically separating the father from the son.[36]

Separation is a concept associated in more than one way with María's difference. Like the figure of the black tresses in Baudelaire's 1857 *Flowers of Evil*, María's tresses are identified both with her ethnic origin and with death itself. In poems like "Hideous Jewess" and "Her Hair," Baudelaire explores the topic of the locket of hair as a memory-laden relic, and as a violent trap. Strands of hair appear separated from the body and the soul in that poetic work, but they also appear as remains of both. Indeed, like the concept of the remainder, the lockets measure the radical separation from both the material form and the divine substance. As Baudelaire puts it, they are the black ocean where the Other hides; the state in between life and death where the Other can still be found; the state of in-betweenness where the Self is tempted to go searching for the Other. María's hair is from the beginning of the novel, and in all pictorial representations of the character, a synecdoche for María herself (fig. 6). At the novel's end her tresses are kept in a coffer. Efraín opens it and screams when they unfurl, appearing to be sensible to his kisses.[37] They have become Baudelairian relics; they represent María's difference, in-betweenness, attractive and repulsive at the same time.

Similarly, María is associated throughout the novel with the classical mythological figure of the Fates (the Moerae in Greek, the Parcae in Roman, and the Norn in Germanic mythology). Linked with both good and evil, these figures stand between newborn life and death, they are the goddesses who both spin and cut the thread of life. They represent death, but they also personify childbirth, and are associated with midwifery. María is similarly represented in the novel as a symbol both for new life and for death. On the

Fig. 6. *Imaginary Portrait of Maria.* By Alejandro Dorronsoro, 1880. In Germán Arciniegas *Genio y figura de Jorge Isaacs* (Buenos Aires: EUDEBA, 1967), 55.

Fig. 7. "Reading Atala by Chateaubriand." Still from the movie *Maria*. In Germán Arciniegas, *Genio y figura de Jorge Isaacs* (Buenos Aires: EUDEBA, 1967), 140–41.

one hand, she is like a white page waiting to be written on: a perfect pupil hanging on Efraín's every word, an eager child with an innocent and pure mind easily imprinted with knowledge.[38] Like Samper's feminine masses, she passively submits to the instruction (or inscription) of the illustrated man. The novel many times returns to this scene of instruction, faithfully depicted by a still from its 1922 movie version (fig. 7).

But the novel also repeats a paradoxical scene in which it is the masculine body that is marked by a deadly feminine agent. The novel's opening provides the first significant example. In the first chapter, the narrator remembers his original separation from his father's house. Ready to follow his father's wishes that he leave his family to study in the capital city of Bogotá, the young Efraín is visited by an unidentified "sister" on the eve of his departure. In a scene that explicitly associates separation with both death and culture, Efraín's sister cuts his hair but remains at home.

There are two other hair cutting scenes in the novel, this time involving not only Efraín, but also his father. The two scenes occur within a few pages

of each other and only a few chapters before Efraín's father suffers a neurasthenic attack that almost kills him. Once again, the reader is reminded of the
Fates, cutting the thread of life, sapping the masculine body of its strength.
But the scenes also remind the reader of Freud's Atropos, not only the agent
of death, but also the origin of culture. It is Efraín's father's decay and eventual demise that will inexorably separate Efraín from his natural origin, from
the house that he turns around to see one last time in the novel's opening
scene, only to see María looking back at him from the window of his mother's
room. A house that stands not only for a lost innocence, but also for an egois-
tic kind of subjectivity unprepared for life's moral challenges.

It makes sense, then, that these scenes also suggest the interiorization of
the feminine principle that María and her mother represent. They are both
self-emasculating scenes, whose symbolic power curiously escapes the male
characters, but is keenly felt by María. Efraín's father himself orders an un-
willing María to cut his hair, while Efraín grants María's "malicious" wish and
cuts the lock of hair himself. In these later scenes, the feminine principle, or
the need for separation, has been interiorized by the virile subject, who does
symbolic violence to himself.

Self-inflicted violence is the consequence of the logic behind the metaphor
that represents the nation as a newborn body contaminated by its feminine
origins. If the nation is like a malleable and indeterminate mass at its origin,
and if that sense of in-betweenness and difference is what is contaminating it,
making it less coherent and less stable; then the nation must do violence to itself, cut off a part of itself, separate itself from the feminine principle that is
inherent to it. Thus, it stands to reason that when Efraín returns to his home
the second time, after a long absence of study in London, he witnesses a dramatic change in his environment. The romantic imagery with which the narrator describes his first return to the Cauca Valley is replaced at the end of
the novel by a seemingly discordant naturalistic account of Efraín's voyage up
the Magdalena river. The account pits Efraín against a natural setting that
has turned unfamiliar and inhospitable; his nostalgic return has turned into a
descent into hell. This transformation makes sense if one takes into account
the changes that Efraín has undergone. Efraín returns as an educated and
cultured citizen, and it stands to reason that he would no longer be welcome
in his once familiar surroundings. Thus, the environment itself seems to be
conspiring against Efraín's return, delaying his trip back, preparing María's
death.[39] It is the countryside itself that seems to delay Efraín's reunion with
María, guaranteeing both her death and his inexorable banishment from
home.

In *María*, Efraín is a virile and traveling subject unified by abstract principles such as citizenship and civil, divine, or paternal law. He is the very opposite of the material and blood-bound, house-bound, feminine Other. But this

virile subject has a hard time keeping himself apart from his sister and mother. Not only was he, after all, once part of a female/maternal body, but he is also the corresponding object of desire of the maternal body, which also has a hard time letting him go. Paradoxically, through this logic, the dangerous feminine Other becomes the very force (internal or external) that cuts off the umbilical cord. The metaphors produced by this logic ultimately suggest a paradoxical equivalence between the civilizing influence and the crisis identified with the feminine principles of difference and with the feminine gendered body.

The Head of State

Like Isaacs and the other members of *El Mosaico*, Samper informs his narrative of original crisis with allusions to the Book of Genesis, though he prefers the Flood to the story of Sarah.[40] Behind the cataclysm, argues Samper, there is a divine plan for a united and stable future. That divinity stands for a unifying principle that runs through Samper's essay. The thrust behind it is the dissemination of a notion of government based on the rule of law, and the inscription and implementation of those laws. The Scriptures, then, are a model and a metaphor for Samper's work, which codifies the laws that must be written and enforced.

The unifying legal principle informing Samper's imagined nation is embodied in a social group of professional men, specifically of lawyers and doctors.[41] Samper distinguishes this group of individuals both from the indistinct indigenous or African masses and from the corrupted Spaniards. The group is, for him, an ambivalent mixture of the biologically determined category of race and the socially determined category of caste. Its members are of Spanish and hence European blood, but they are also marked by their individualism and by their extensive education. They are *letrados criollos*, educated creole men, mostly different from the mechanical and instinct-driven masses.[42]

This group, described as the "head" of the social "body," is responsible for "heroically" intervening on the body-mass, either by "imprinting" it with their ideas, or by "operating" on it to excise the carcinogenic principle.[43] The metaphorical imprinting of ideas on "the people," wrote Samper, would turn revolutions into mere insurrections, and would erase the dualism that plagued the period of Spanish colonization.[44] Samper's choice of words here is religiously precise. Revolution and duality are traditionally associated with crisis, with the Fall of man, Original Sin, and the subsequent creation of the duality of good and evil. Samper opposes revolution and duality to insurrection and unity, which in turn are associated with rising, Resurrection, and with the divine and mysterious unity of the Godhead. These traditionally gender-coded associations are central to Samper's work. They determine his representation of the future nation's unquestionably masculine form, as well as its necessary separation from a feminine revolutionary principle: the metaphorical weaning of the educated child from the maternal body.[45]

Weaning, however, is a painful process, which seems to compound the pleasure felt by Samper from the inscription of the feminine body, judging by his metaphorical representation of that education as invasive and penetrating. Not surprisingly, Samper argues that the education of the body-mass is accompanied by instructive pains.[46] Similarly, the expression of sadness worn by all of the icons representing María, in Isaacs's novel, is a reference not only to her fate, but also to the pain that comes with the changes literally operated on her. Indeed, pain in the novel is not only a necessary side effect of civilizing treatment, it even becomes the necessary precondition for all change and improvement.[47] Both in the novel and in Samper's political essay, pain is an index of the dimension of the intervention that is necessary to wipe the slate clean, to begin again, to give birth to a new man.[48] The necessity of pain, however, gives a paradoxical corporeality to the educated man, who now seems to follow the principle of reproduction. By its own logic, pain suggests that the civilizing influence associated by both authors with the letter, the law, and writing, has erased and replaced the female body with an analogous body that produces crises in its own right.

The Queen of Hearts

Isaacs's coming-of-age novel deploys and further develops this precarious metaphorical network around the reproductive body. He dramatically opens the novel with a dedication to his metaphorical brothers (Isaacs's admirers from the gentleman's club *El Mosaico*, no doubt) whose first line emphasizes change: "My dear friends, here is the story of adolescence of the one whom you loved so dearly, and who is no longer." The dedication is but one of many allusions in the novel to the temporal schism that separates the narrator not only from his father's house, from his mother, and from María, but also from his past, from his younger, adolescent self. Indeed, the novel juxtaposes Efraín's youthful appearance with his expected development into a rational gentleman, dramatizing in this way the transition from a puerile to a virile Efraín.

Not surprisingly, the prologue and the beginning of the novel both focus on Efraín's mind and head (on his feverish disposition and on his flowing hair). Such emphasis continues throughout the novel, which later shows him as a studious reader.[49] Indeed, the lesson Efraín must learn is how to detach himself rationally from his body, from his tendency to be overly sentimental, from his emotional nature, even from his sexual desires, in order to gain the confidence of all of those around him. Such confidence will accord Efraín the respect and authority he needs to become the future head of his own family, as well as the successful heir to his father's estate.

Efraín's goals, however, are paradoxically at odds with the steps necessary to reach them. Efraín's liberal education clearly elevates him to a higher moral ground, spiritualizes him, and gives him a moral compass evident in his principled objections to the cruelty of slavery. But education also seems to feminize Efraín, a fate that characters fear throughout the novel. It is clear to the characters in the novel, for example, that a city education is at odds with the development of the physical strength necessary to succeed in the Colombian countryside. It is, in fact, a mystery to Efraín's friend Carlos how a liberal arts education (composed of heterogeneous readings ranging from the Bible to *Don Quixote*) will contribute to the family's fortune. In an often-quoted letter written from Bogotá (the city of Efraín's education) two years after the novel was published, even Isaacs describes the effect of the city on himself in similar terms: "city life feminizes, degrades and diminishes one," he writes.[50]

Isaacs's paradoxical anxiety about the feminizing influence of an extensive education in a modern city is shared by his contemporaries. It results in the literary figure of the *cachaco* common to several of the articles of customs and manners published in the four-volume *Museo*.[51] The *cachaco* is the Colombian version of the European *dandy*. It is one word at the center of a constellation of terms including *gomoso, lechuguino, petimetre, currutaco, pisaverde*, all of which make reference to varying forms of the feminine principle of difference that undermines the subject's masculinity: an excessive concern with physical appearance, a disregard for the truth, a tendency to dissimulate, to perform an act, to appear to be that which one is not. The term *gomoso* is particularly interesting from this perspective because it means to have the qualities of rubber (*goma*), a substance in between a solid and a liquid, whose viscosity and tendency to flow are its defining characteristics. Moreover, *goma* also refers to a brain tumor of syphilitic origin, combining in one disease the gendered opposites of body and mind. Not surprisingly, then, a *cachaco* is represented as both a young man studying to be a doctor or a lawyer, and as a mama's boy, born from his mother's womb already dressed with the ostentatious cassock that distinguishes him.[52] This ostentation not only undermines his masculinity, but also depletes his patrimony: the wealth resulting from his father's hard work and economy. Most important, in all of these representations of the *cachaco*, the depletion is not only allowed, but is even unexplainably encouraged by the father himself.

Similarly, in *María*, both Efraín and his father suffer the ill consequences of the commitment to Efraín's education. After Efraín's father's neurasthenic collapse from his financial worries, it is fairly clear that Efraín's education will cost the family economy too much. And yet, despite the city's ill effects on Efraín, and in spite of the risk and sacrifice that such weakening represents to Efraín and to his family, his father remains stubbornly committed to completing his education with a six-year tenure in Europe. As if moved by a similarly mysterious will to degenerate, Efraín accommodates his father, over María's protests. Efraín's tendency to degenerate is further suggested by his frequent lachrymose spells, his passionate self-indulgence, and his tendency toward solitude. It is most clearly manifested in Efraín's attraction to his cousin, and in his defiant determination to face all of the consequences of his marriage to María, against the doctor's apparently sound advice.

Off with His Head!

Isaacs's simultaneous attraction to repulsion by the feminine principle of difference is perhaps best represented by the scene of the tiger hunt. The elaborate scene is divided into two parts, and has two separate endings. Efraín, asked by his father to get a bearskin for his bedroom, instead goes on a tiger hunt with José and Braulio, faithful "mulatto" workers who own small properties on Efraín's father's estate. The first part of the hunt is unpredictable, unstaged, and dangerous. The tiger is wounded by José and Braulio, but still kills a number of the hunting dogs. It almost kills Braulio, when Efraín fortuitously shoots it in the head, turning him into the hero of the expedition. After the hunt, Braulio skins the tiger, cuts off its head, and puts it inside a bag. The bag is opened twice in two subsequent family scenes whose staged quality makes them different from the more improvised first part of the hunt.

First, the decapitated head is displayed to José's family. The moment inspired the most striking of the charcoal drawings illustrating the novel's 1882 edition (fig. 8). The illustration shows José dramatically holding up the bloody trophy of the hunt, displaying the hole in the tiger's forehead, but curiously looking away from the viewer. The reader, however, knows that Efraín killed the tiger. Details of the drawing, such as the bullet hole and José's looking askance, are meant to call attention to that fact. José's wife and daughters, Doña Luisa, Tránsito, and Lucía, all scream when José shows them the bloody head, and they turn to look at Efraín. He, in turn, sits on a stool (provided for effect by Braulio) commanding the scene of terror.

The second scene happens soon after. Efraín stealthily returns to his house, secretly entering his bedroom, invisible to everyone but his mother. He sends his "page" (Juan Angel, a visually black character like José) into the dining room with the bag. Efraín's father orders Juan Angel to display its

Fig. 8. *The Head of the Tiger.* By Alejandro Riquer. In Jorge Isaacs, *Maria: novela americana* (Barcelona: Arte y letras, 1882), p. 109. Benson Latin American Collection, University of Texas at Austin.

contents, thinking that the bag contains pieces of quartz. When Juan Angel opens the bag, he realizes what is inside, drops it, and screams, "The tiger!" Everyone freezes. Efraín's father walks over to the bag, shakes it fearfully, and watches in horror as the head rolls out over the flagstones. Stepping back, he screams, "It's monstrous!" As before, everyone's thoughts turn to Efraín. His mother forgets she has seen him; María looks to the hills, searching for him with anguish. Mayo (the faithful dog) freezes, and then runs madly around the house, howling and instinctively sensing that something has happened to Efraín. Suddenly, Efraín enters the scene, announced by the four-year-old who exclaims, "Here's the bogey-man!" During the commotion, Efraín has changed his clothes, and now appears "dressed in a suit that would have made him unrecognizable to Tránsito and Lucía." Once again, he commands the scene; his composure and elegance contrast with the chaos that reigns in the dining room, relieving all those gathered from their worst fear.[53]

Both scenes in which the tiger's head is displayed, as well as the illustration that accompanies them, are staged in more ways than one. Not only are they artificially built around dramatic entrances, heroic gestures, and props skillfully manipulated; the scenes also make pointed references to the myth of Perseus and the Medusa's head. The decapitation, the bag for the severed head, the visibility and invisibility of the hero, the indirect glance, the freezing and horrific effect of the display, are all either props or events common to both stories.

More significantly, the necessary relationship between the coming of age of the hero and patricide is implied both by the myth and by the hunt. This connection partly answers the question about the origins of the mysterious tendency to degenerate that operates in the novel. Like Perseus, Efraín is a hero who faces a deadly test of his manhood put to him by a patriarchal figure. It is both a test of his strength and a test of his allegiance to the principle of singularity. But it is that same principle that finds it necessary to put Efraín's life in jeopardy. The principle of singularity, carried to its logical extreme, requires the death of the son or the father. As in the myth, Efraín's allegiance to the paternal law carries with it the paradoxical and symbolic decapitation of the father. Efraín's father, like King Polydectes of Seriphus and his court in the Medusa myth, suffers the consequences of maintaining his singular authority. Putting the sons to the test, the patriarchs end up with more than they bargained for. Like Perseus, Efraín rises to the challenge, and gains the respect of everyone around him. He violently changes positions with the patriarch. He seems to turn into a man by penetrating the tiger and spilling its blood. His gain in stature appears to be in direct correlation to his father's loss of face in the moment of terror. In Nietzschean terms, the will and means to a greater power is achieved at the expense of lesser powers. Progress depends on degeneration.

But authority further depends on overcoming the catastrophic fear of Efraín's own death. Like "necessary pain" in Samper's political essay, Efraín's death is an index of the radical gesture necessary to wipe the slate clean. To begin anew, Efraín scares his father and his family by staging the possibility of his own death, thereby hinting that the family is headless. From this perspective, the tiger's severed head is a reminder of Efraín's eviration and feminization. The decapitated head of the tiger is a signifier for Efraín's own severed head and for his missing body. Not surprisingly, everyone looks for Efraín's body upon the head's display.

The tiger's head is then reminiscent of the myth of Medusa, artfully and indirectly deployed by Efraín, a metaphor for the necessary self-obliteration of the singularity principle: the required move from head of state to head-less state, from masculine head to feminine body. It stands for the experience of absolute loss deemed necessary by these authors to believe in their nation's recovery.[54] To read *María* and the *Ensayo* is to feel a kinship with the degenerating virile subject, or with the *letrado*. These fraternal ties to Efraín and his brothers precipitate a shared fall from a divine masculine world of substance. which predisposes this select brotherhood to believe in Paradise regained.

Conclusion

In this chapter, I have examined the engendering of crisis and its consequences. After tracing a genealogy of degeneration, the nineteenth-century crisis that constitutes the foundation of Samper and Isaacs's metaphorical network, I hope to have established the identification not only between degeneration and the reproductive body of women, but also between degeneration and a virile subjectivity. Then I studied specific metaphors that emerge from Isaacs's and Samper's network of crisis and gender, focusing on the paradoxes that these networks and their metaphors produce: one is the male consciousness that willfully degenerates or inflicts violence on itself, another is the female body that is both the danger (as crypt of nature) and the hope (as origin of culture) of that subject.

Perhaps the principal paradox whose various forms I have here attempted to trace is the transformation of life into death. The paradox is the necessary result of a logic of ascent or progress based on the separation from a point of critical origin, at the center of which both Isaacs and Samper place a feminine reproductive body. According to this logic, the contaminated (male) Self not only must separate itself from its deadly origin, but his progress becomes contingent on overcoming, or inflicting violence, on that part of himself that is contaminated, that must decay. To do so, however, is also to kill the body of the Self, to return to the point of departure, to death. Perhaps Freud put it best when he said that, despite his apparently rebellious choice, King Lear really has no choice at all. He must always choose Cordelia, Atropos incarnate.

But Freudian figures like Atropos and Medusa have more recently been interpreted by Freud's own careful readers as metaphors that displace (cover up and expose) the apparently logical processes that construct such truths.[55] Following these readings, the duality principle embodied in reproduction and in its many figures also stands for a kind of seeing that is equivalent with interpretation. Indeed, the figure of Medusa's head saves us from the danger of thinking that we see dead on. It exposes the mechanism through which we claim to see truth directly, and calls into question not only the notion of seeing, but also the very notion of truth. To use the figure of Medusa's head is then to call truth unwittingly into question by giving the reader the means to his or her own reading.

By the same token, the figure raises the philosophical question of government and self-government. If the crisis of the national Self is embedded in its very reproduction, and in the eternal return of difference that such reproduction signifies, what must its government look like?[56] If government is already inscribed in the description of the national Self, then what notion of government rules over a national body represented, or seen, as a body whose very reproduction is critical? There is no right answer to these questions, of course. The very notion of government through inscription becomes a paradox when representation or writing have the same apparent effect as reproduction: multiplying meaning, doubling the Self, splitting the hairs of truth.

Not surprisingly, Isaacs's novel underscores the artifice that both covers and props up the logic that produces these paradoxes. Let us return to the scene where Efraín, like Perseus, shows a facsimile of the head of Medusa. In that scene, Efraín's death is pointedly staged; it is as fabricated an act as his authority. The well-dressed Efraín who comes out of his room to everyone's relief and surprise, is a bogeyman. He is a make-believe character in a children's story meant to discipline the imagination. The story suggests that if a virile subjectivity lies at the core of the logic of ascent, that subjectivity is also a child playing at death. Such moments, compared by Nietzsche to dancing, depend on being "light" on one's feet. They are the liberating scenes of interpretation that counteract the "heaviness" of so-called truths like the birth of nations, or the heads of state.

Anemia, Witches, and Vampires

FIGURES TO GOVERN THE COLONY

Introduction

In order to constitute themselves as the governing authority of the emerging Puerto Rican nation before the United States' invasion in 1898, a group of *letrados* constructed the phantasm of a coherent and integrated national Self by excluding a phantasmagoric Other (e.g., the infirm Puerto Rican *jíbaro*).[1] A close examination of the works by this educated elite makes apparent the complexity of the dynamic between discourses of the Self and the Other that sustain this act of empowerment.

In this essay, I examine the relationship not only between the *letrado's* discourse of Self and its phantasmagoric Other, but also between the *letrado's* discourse of Self and competing discourses of Self similarly articulated by the changing metropolitan authorities (Spanish first and North American later).[2] These metropolitan discourses of Self were articulated against a "black" body "seen" even within the body of the *letrado*.[3] For reasons of political expediency, the members of the privileged elite found themselves both accepting and refining this opposition. This negotiated solution, however, would lead to a strategy of displacement based on an interiorized fear of their own bodies, which is simultaneously concealed and revealed in some of the cultural artifacts produced between 1880 and 1904 to construct the Puerto Rican nation.

In short, I will show that the empowerment by a group of *letrados* is what motivates the deployment of a set of devices that, paradoxically, feeds the fear of miscegenation. The members of this group need to displace the threat their own bodies pose to the local colonial authorities, which leads to the representation of the "black" body as a contaminating parasite that must be eliminated, and to the representation of the "white" peasant woman's body as invaded by a curable disease.

The anemic body of the peasant woman appeared most prominently in the literary and scientific works of Salvador Brau, a sociologist, and Francisco del Valle Atiles, a hygienist, two writers associated with the professional class of liberal reformists.[4] In my analysis of their works, I hope to show that the figure of the anemic peasant woman was the result of a significant adjustment of the figure of the vagrant peasant (an earlier phantasm). Vagrancy, and the related condition of promiscuity, were moral and economic qualities attributed to the indigenous population of the colony by the local colonial administrators. This condition was understood to be determined by environmental as well as by hereditary factors. It was constructed by the colonial authorities in an effort to establish the need for violent order and control of the colony with devices similar in kind to those deployed to support the institution of slavery. Vagrancy posed a problem for the *letrado*, however, because it applied as easily to the peasant as it did to himself.

From the metropolitan perspective, the abolition of slavery in 1873 made less tenable the violent methods used to maintain social and political order by the local colonial authorities. They sought a more indirect method of control. The *letrados* offered public health, and public health education, as less violent devices for control. From the perspective of the *letrados*, the changing political climate made possible the challenge to the figure of the vagrant peasant, which they replaced with a new figurative network: a state of normative illness. This network, perhaps first articulated by Salvador Brau in 1882, modernized the paradigmatic constructions of the metropolis and was used against the local administrators. It included the parasite and the anemic "white" peasant woman, even as it displaced the threat of difference and danger posed by their own bodies to the metropolitan administration. With the figure of the parasite, they displaced this difference onto the "black" body, constructed as a different biological life form. With the figure of anemia, they displaced the site of the struggle on to the body of the peasant woman. This body then served as a buffer zone that kept the "white" virile body of the *letrado* above the fray.

Analyzing the constructs of this educated elite will help us understand the role played by representatives of the new laboratory medicine, some of whom entered the island with the invading forces of 1898.[5] Comparing the work of these scientists with the work of the *letrados* will suggest the importance of the constructs of the anemic peasant woman, and of the parasite, as points of departure for the governing practices of the new metropolitan authority.

Constructing Vagrancy

The 1880s were marked by social and political turmoil in Puerto Rico. From an economic perspective, the worldwide overproduction of sugar led to changes in the Puerto Rican economy, which was dependent on this product even after the abolition of slavery in 1873. The Puerto Rican agricultural system moved away from sugar production, dependent on slave labor, to coffee production, dependent on paid labor. Along with these economic changes came a demographic movement from the cities and plains to the mountains of Puerto Rico, and a concomitant fragmentation of family units.[6] Changes in the state of public health also accompanied these shifts, leading to an increase in the mortality rate of peasants; they affected more than peasants, as well. The epidemics of yellow fever, which multiplied during this decade to the point of having an epidemic declared almost every two years, struck and killed two Spanish governors.[7]

This flux in economic, demographic, and health registers brought to a head a series of political confrontations between the liberal progressive forces of professional *letrados* (with affiliations to the land-owning classes), and the conservatives in control of the colonial government. These two social groups had been vying for political power throughout the nineteenth century, and had last come to a violent confrontation in 1868, when the liberal uprising was summarily and successfully squelched by the conservative forces of the colonial state. Significantly, however, this decade ended with both a more radicalized and stronger liberal pro-autonomy party, and with the forced resignation of Spanish governor-general Palacios, after his attempt to control the better-organized liberals through a policy of repression.[8] In fact, it is a historical commonplace that the changes that occurred during this decade prepared the political landscape for the short-lived autonomous state instituted in 1898.

A public debate on education stood as a crucial moment of liberal empowerment and definition against a misinformed and unreasonable colonial authority. In 1880 the Spanish governor-general Eulogio Despujol argued that the greatest obstacle to Puerto Rican progress was the lack of morally constituted families in the countryside. Moreover, he argued that because of the ongoing mobility of the Puerto Rican peasant, and, most important, owing to the base nature of the Puerto Rican peasant woman (whose body was dominated by an instinctive "lack of moral restraint"), education was not a solution to the problem:

> I find myself in agreement with the principle of establishing rural schools for girls. Disseminated in isolated hovels, lacking in religious instruction and in moral restraint, without either the Sacrament or the rule of Law to legitimize many,

more or less lasting unions, created on the sole and unstable basis of sensual appetite, it can indeed be said that the family, in the Puerto Rican countryside, is not morally constituted, which represents the principal obstacle to its future progress. It is easy, then, to understand how important it would be to educate women in the primary knowledge of reading and writing . . . [and in] the notions of religion and morality . . . [But] today, that same moral laxity, and the daily transit of precocious children of both sexes, ages nine to twelve, from their hovels to distant schools, through wandering roads, are . . . evils which will destroy, or at least overcome, the moralizing effects of rural education.[9]

Despujol's argument against public education presupposed a biological proximity between the "black" body and the Puerto Rican peasant body. He suggested a closeness between the body of the female peasant and the "black" body at two different levels. At one level, he suggested that if the female peasant stepped outside her house, she would run into an unspecified "evil." Readers of Despujol's text would know how to interpret this evil force. The peasant's "isolation," their "hovels," and their "wandering roads," assembled to create a familiar figurative stage that determined the meaning of the evil. Surrounding the imagined house the reader saw a thick and dangerous tropical environment, whose vegetable life, according to contemporary scientific knowledge, was equivalent to the dangerous life form of the "black" body.[10] Despujol also suggested that the body of the Puerto Rican peasant woman was biologically close to the body of the newly freed slaves. For Despujol, the Puerto Rican peasant woman was at a primitive stage of the Great Chain of Being. References to her "lack of moral restraint," "precociousness," and "sensual appetite" placed her closer to the predominantly physical and irrational animal than to the thinking, morally constituted European. According to the scientific discourse of the time, this put her next to the "African race," which also occupied the lower rungs of the evolutionary scale.[11] Like those of newly freed slaves, the peasant woman's body was seen as physiologically condemned to promiscuity, a kind of genetic sexual vagrancy. This biological and environmental argument, combined with the historical precedent set by the revolution of former slaves in Haiti, made Spanish governors like Despujol suspicious of the merits of public education.

Implied in Despujol's argument was also the repetition of earlier repressive and violent practices used to control a peasant population that was, for him, ultimately beyond regeneration. Historically, the military colonial state had used a different version of the environmental argument to increase productivity through the control of movement. I am referring to the environmental argument wielded by colonial administrators like Miguel de la Torre (1822–1837), Miguel López de Baños (1838–1841), and Juan de la Pezuela (1848–1851) to justify a repressive system of control. These governor-generals used the allusions made in eighteenth-century histories and travel accounts to the island's excessively benign tropical environment to construct the figure of the Puerto Rican vagrant peasant. Later they used this figure to justify the creation of a sacro-municipal institution and of a device to supervise and discipline the conduct and movement of the vagrant body. Governor-generals established a board on vagrancy and cohabitation for that purpose, and created the device of "the notebook," styled after the Napoleonic *livret*, which the worker was forced to carry with him, and which had to be regularly presented for inspection to the authorities.[12]

By 1873, however, the metropolitan government already considered these repressive methods of discipline and punishment to be ineffective. After the abolition of slavery in Puerto Rico, the local authorities attempted to reinstate the practice of the notebook, but the metropolitan government disapproved. Significantly, the argument the Spanish metropolitan government used against reestablishing this system was that, like slavery, it led to an "unsustainable social state, which would lead to mutiny and serious conflict in the public order."[13] In that same document the metropolitan government stated that "[the] only thing that can be admitted in the present situation in which the Island finds itself, are either measures of policing and prevention of incursions against the public order or indirect practices of Government and Administration."[14]

Despite this suggestion by the metropolitan government, the local and municipal authorities still wielded repressive measures by the third quarter of the nineteenth century.[15] Indeed, Despujol's categorical denial of the benefits of public education could be understood as one such example. His description of the Puerto Rican peasant woman as promiscuous and vagrant suggested to the *letrados* a possible return to repressive practices such as the notebook system. Moreover, the proximity between the "black" body and the body of the Puerto Rican peasant presupposed by Despujol's words must have suggested to the *letrados* that in the eyes of the local colonial government there was no difference between the promiscuous "black race," the unruly peasant, and the "creole" upstarts. Thus, they must have feared that these violent practices would be wielded against them, too. Finally, the uncompromising position of the colonial authority on public education provided the *letrados* with an opportunity to intervene in the spirit of the recommendations made by the metropolitan government.

The *Letrado* Analysis

In their scientific works, manuals of hygiene, naturalist literature, and essays, *letrados* like Atiles and Brau confronted the discourse of the colonial administration with a discourse only slightly changed, and with a set of disciplinary practices revised to fit better the description set forth by the metropolitan authorities. By so doing, they authorized themselves as a more legitimate and effective colonial government. A concern with productivity, for example, continued to be at the center of the emergent discourse, and how best to harness the excess of energy represented by vices such as promiscuity and gambling was still the concern of the powerful group of *letrados*. But now the *letrados* emphasized their difference from the dangerous figure of a "black" body, and placed it at the center of these related problems.

The new discourse altered the central players of the colonial drama. Thus, the *letrados* substituted the state of widespread vagrancy, determined by the sacro-legal Board of Vagrancy and Cohabitation, for a state of normative illness, which would eventually take the form of tropical anemia, or urcinariasis, and would be determined by the medico-legal Board of Health, headed by the hygienist. This substitution depended on the new scientific knowledge about the environment. The older scientific paradigm, which saw only a benign tropical environment, was replaced with a newer scientific version of the tropics as a source of ill health. The new discourse also changed the practice of government. Following the analysis of the metropolitan administration, the new discipline was no longer "direct." Mediation now became the key concept, and public health education became the new controlling device.

This double agenda of accommodation to the metropolitan decree and empowerment of the *letrados* led Brau and Atiles to confront the danger posed by their self-perceived racial difference with two strategies. On the one hand, Atiles and Brau opposed the new European environmental argument presented by local administrators like Despujol. They argued that the tropical climate did not lead inevitably to a race with predominantly "black" traits.[16] Atiles argued that, in fact, the "African race" had never ruled the island. Following the theory of degeneration outlined by Edward Long in his *History of Jamaica* (1774), he even argued that the eventual sterility of the former slaves was assured.[17] Brau, an abolitionist, did not openly predict the eventual disappearance of the former slaves, but he suggested their contribution to the "creole race" was negligible when he claimed that the organic elements attributed to the "European race" predominated in the racial makeup of the Puerto Rican nation.[18]

On the other hand, both Atiles and Brau differentiated between the dangerous "black" body and an innocent "white" peasant population, or *jíbaros*. This difference was suggested by comparing the "black" body of the former slave to both a metaphorical and a discrete disease, while the peasant body was compared to the innocent victim of disease. The construction of illness as a metaphor for the "African race" was gradual. Brau took the first step, which was to make illness into a metaphor for the precarious state of the Puerto Rican nation.

Illness as a Metaphor[19]

Brau's contribution to the reconfiguration of the threat posed by the "white" body of the "creole" or *criollo* was his direct challenge to the figure of the vagrant peasant that he carried out in his scientific memoir "The Working Classes" (1882). In this foundational text, Brau set out to question the repressive practices of the local authorities, and specifically the practice of the notebook, by arguing that the apparent delinquent vagrancy of the Puerto Rican peasant was in fact the consequence of the repressive disciplinary strategies, or excesses, of the colonial administration.

For Brau, the mistaken label of vagrancy hid the actual reality of colonial abuse; which he referred to as a disease. Using the metaphor of the anatomist, diagnosing a social problem, Brau argued that the weakened state of the *jíbaro* was due to the living conditions under a repressive colonial administration.[20] These conditions, he argued, made the peasant rebellious. But even more than the conditions themselves, the practices meant to put down the rebellion of the peasant (imprisonment and exile) made the problem worse. Brau argued that these repressive practices created invisible, isolated, and dangerous spaces of confrontation, inaccessible to the colonial administration.

Moreover, imprisonment and exile had the added effect of leaving the Puerto Rican peasant woman unsupervised.[21] Together with other liberal reformists, he suggested that this lack of supervision led to interracial mixing.[22] Thus, at the center of the invisible space created by the repressive policies of the colonial administration, Brau placed the abandoned body of the female peasant, whose integrity was threatened by the newly gained mobility of freed slaves.

The center of this invisible space was perhaps best described in Brau's naturalist short novel ¿*Sinner*? (1887). In this novel, the miserable natures of both the ruling classes and the working classes combine to determine the fate of Cocola, a peasant woman who dies after being raped by a young member of the upper class. She is accused of vagrancy by the local authorities, and the story tells of the attempts by a doctor to redeem her memory after her death by addressing the real problem. To do so, the doctor visits the unknown countryside of Puerto Rico, the space that remained invisible to both the urban population and the colonial authorities.[23] At the center of this space, the doctor finds the moral corruption of figures of authority, as well as an example of the physiological cause underlying the uncivilized state of the Puerto Rican worker.

The central scene of the short novel is a representation of vice and unharnessed sexuality in a church, where preparations are being made for a burial. The description of the scene underscores both the moral corruption of the local figures of municipal authority and the physical corruption of the peasants. While Brau reveals the moral corruption of the municipal authority by the fact that the funeral is for the concubine of a government official, he suggests the physical corruption of the peasants by referring to the ubiquity of "black" bodies in the church. He represents all of the "blacks" in the scene as diseased, weak, and ignorant, and their movement as excessive and inappropriate, bringing them dangerously close to the "white" members of the congregation. The excess of their movement, and the danger of their proximity, is suggested by the selection and description of two instruments producing the raucous music played during the funeral. The first is a *bombardino*, a hornlike instrument traditionally associated with African rhythms and "black" performers.[24] The second instrument is an organ, whose player is shadowed by a figure described as "tall, black as ink, with scarce flesh on his bones, and of a delinquent physiognomy."[25] Brau summarizes these combined references to the irreverence, delinquency, and thus the danger of the ubiquitous "black" body in the image that closes the passage:

> Maybe upon seeing them a pessimistic observer would have been able to make hay of [the scene's] satirical content, supposing that the destructive worms of that human waste pulp called cadaver, had not waited this time for the decomposition of the prey, but had given free reign to their voracity.[26]

The image compares the scene's vagrant "black" bodies to worms consuming a cadaver. The comparison expands upon Brau's use of illness as a metaphor for abuse by a colonial authority to include also the perceived problem of miscegenation. A peasant body, first weakened and then abandoned by the colonial administration, finally dies and decomposes. Given the context of this passage, it is fairly clear that the decomposition stands as a metaphor for degeneration, or for the effect of the "African race" on the abandoned Puerto Rican peasant. Thus, Brau suggested in his work that the excesses of the colonial administration set up the conditions that made possible the degeneration of the Puerto Rican race. He suggested that the undesirable physical consequences of the closeness between these qualitatively different bodies resulted from the misguided governing practices of the local administration. The Puerto Rican peasant woman fell prey to the newly freed slave only after being permanently damaged by repeated colonial mistreatment. In this way Brau questioned Despujol's assumption that the body of the Puerto Rican peasant woman (and, by extension, the body of the *criollo*), was genetically equivalent to the body of the slave.

Illness as a Metaphor for the "Black" Body

This scene of degeneration was clearly an inspiration for Francisco Oller, a Puerto Rican painter, and also a member of the *letrado* class. In his 1893 painting *The Wake*, Oller turned illness into a metaphor for the "black" body (fig. 9). The painting is divided into three distinct spaces, which I will discuss separately. The first space is held by the figure of a weak, poorly dressed, "black" figure, and by a dead child. The poverty of the standing figure is suggested by his ragged clothes and by his walking stick, a prop used by Oller in his 1881 portrait of a beggar (fig. 10). In both paintings, Oller used the walking stick to signify poverty and vagrancy.

Two things establish a common space between the vagrant "black" figure and the dead child. First, the "black" figure looks directly at the child, and second, like the dead child, he is oblivious to the revelry that surrounds them. Moreover, like the dead child, he seems frozen, existing in a time different from that which defines the quick gestures of the rest of the company. The image is powerful. It links death to the emaciated "black" body in what seems like a visitation directly from the underworld. The sense of

Fig. 9. *The Wake, 1893.* By Francisco Oller. Photograph by Jochi Melero. In *Francisco Oller A Realist Impressionist.* (Ponce: Museo de Arte de Ponce, 1983), 144. From the original belonging to the collection of the Museum of History, Anthropology and Art of the University of Puerto Rico.

sacrilegious visitation is further emphasized by the mockery of a crucifixion held high above the head of the "black" figure, a suggestion of a new unholy trinity.

The second space is set by the diagonal line of people from the open door center right to the left margin of the painting. It stands as an allegory for degeneration, therapeutically ordering its unharnessed energies. While it first appears to be a chaotic mixture of races, genders, and ages, upon closer examination it reveals a specific order. It shows a processional scene of revelry, which includes three groups, each one representing a different level of vice and unrestrained energy. The group immediately to the left of the standing figure is made up of singers, musicians, and drinking peasants colored both white and black. Their violence is suggested by the gesture of the "white" peasant holding his machete. This group is followed by another of three figures in a violent embrace, whose sexual force is suggested by the alcohol poured on the heads of two of the figures. On the floor we find the final group, representing a scene of destruction. It is made up of three children, two colored white and one black. The "black" child is made invisible by the detritus surrounding it, and by its inverted fetal position; but it clearly represented the final consequence of the serpentine line of vice and miscegenation circumscribed by the second space.

The third space is contained by the open green door and the right margin of the painting. It consists of a small group of characters, all of them "white," including two figures representing the colonial authority: a priest and a frightened older representative of the state. Together with three other "white" figures, they surround a "white" peasant woman, ineffectively seeking to protect her from the mayhem. The sensation of imminent violence between the second and third space is suggested by a second figure reaching for a machete. The violent interaction between these two spaces is further emphasized by the gaze of the men who make up the third group. They look past the central scene of the painting, focusing instead on the scene across from them. The position of the two figures of colonial authority is of special importance here. While the hand of the priest misses a wine glass offered by the peasant woman, the cowering representative of the state moves away from her. The movement of these figures suggests the abandonment of the body of the peasant woman by a distracted and fearful state and church. Like the peasant woman discussed in Brau's work, this figure is alone and abandoned. Like the "black" figure at the painting's center, she is invisible, set apart from the group that surrounds her, standing in a kind of void, disconnected from, oblivious to, and, most important, ignored by her surroundings.

On the other hand, the direction of the gaze of the men in the group emphasizes the direction of the peasant woman's stare. She too is distracted. Clearly the glass she is about to give to the priest will soon shatter on the floor. But her distraction is different from that of the men surrounding her. She is not distracted by the sacrilegious or violent nature of the scene in front of her. Instead, she smiles innocently and stares blankly in the direction of an invisible viewer as if inviting him or her in. Indeed, the outward direction of the peasant woman's gaze sets up an invisible triangular structure in which the viewer plays a distinct part. Her welcoming gaze displaces the viewer's attention away from the central "black" figure, who occupies the inevitable and threatening space where a viewer's gaze would otherwise rest. As the viewer's gaze is moved off to the side, a paradoxical space between the two figures is created. On the one hand, a common space arises, connecting these two figures and suggesting miscegenation as the hidden cause of the infant's death. But on the other hand, a space of difference also emerges between the vagrant "black" figure and the figure of the peasant woman.

The painting, then, makes illness into a metaphor for the "black" body. Illness appears in the painting in the form of racial degeneration. Degeneration is represented as a "black" child in the fetal position at the painting's edge, which results from a degenerating line of bodies. It also appears as a voracious vagrant "black" figure standing over the dead child, which the painting offers to him as a sacrificial victim to be devoured. In his painting, Oller displaces the threat of illness in the peasant woman's body, and in the body of the *letrado* viewing and diagnosing the painting. Instead, he firmly situates illness in the "black" figure.

Anemia's Figurative Network

While Brau and Oller used illness as a metaphor to displace the dangerous difference away from the "white" body of the *letrado*, and to empower their privileged class, Francisco del Valle Atiles used the construct of anemia to accomplish the same ends. In his 1887 scientific memoir, Atiles agrees with Brau's representation of the Puerto Rican peasant. Like Brau, Atiles argues that the colonial authorities made a mistake when they described the peasant as both "vagrant" and "promiscuous." Like the sociologist, Atiles offers a different interpretation of the condition of the Puerto Rican peasant population, presenting them, instead, as the victims of a colonial administration that had abused and abandoned them. Also like Brau, Atiles argues that the excessive force used by the colonial administration has driven the peasants out of sight, into the forests of Puerto Rico, where they become both invisible and ill.

Atiles distinguished himself from Brau, however, in his use of a clinical model, with which he transformed the figurative diseased state of the nation into the visible and discrete disease of tropical anemia. Anemia was a convenient disease construct for a class of *letrados* concerned with the issue of miscegenation. It literally means "want of blood" in the original Greek, and as such it was a useful figure for the *letrado*'s concern with the peasant woman's loss of "good" or "pure" (read "white") blood.

According to the hygienics discourse on tropical anemia, blood was lost principally through contamination or extraction by parasites. Atiles invoked two different theories to construct this figure. On the one hand, he referred to the theory of parasitic infection, which claimed that disease was caused by the penetration of a living agent into a healthy organism. Following this theory, the Cuban physician Carlos Juan Finlay suggested in 1882 that the *Aedes aegipti* mosquito was a carrier for the parasite that caused yellow fever. Manipulating Finlay's findings, Atiles made the parasite and the mosquito into equivalent causes of anemia in his 1883 article "Against Miasma."

> We live in a country whose principal scourge is the climate. However, climate is in part modifiable: and in Puerto Rico the enervating tropical heat, alternating with tremendous rain showers, would be more bearable if there were no swamps,

whose miasmas, especially at night, fly like vampires to steal, treacherously, the blood and the life of the inhabitants of our rural areas. Let us rid ourselves of the swamps, and the air will not be contaminated by the gaseous secretions of so many cadavers that fall prey to yellow fever; let us rid ourselves of them, and we will make disappear the profound anemia that turns peasants into literal skins of water, inert and useless to the land that feeds us.[27]

The fantastic and well-known figure of the vampire served Atiles to reconcile the parasitic theory with the conflicting miasmatic theory of disease, according to which diseases such as anemia were caused by vaporous exhalations from dying organic matter. The figure of the vampire was both like the parasite (not dead), and like miasma (not alive). By comparing the mosquito to a vampire, Atiles suggested its own peculiar life form. The mosquito was born in the swamp. It nourished itself with the swamp's contaminated waters and odors, living at night. The mosquito was saturated with the swamp's virus, which it injected into the blood of healthy organisms, thus transforming them through contamination into something like themselves. Moreover, Atiles underscored the invisibility of the mosquito, which, like a vampire, moved unseen from place to place, performing its blood exchange, replacing life with its own bad blood.

Atiles's concern with an invisible life form that exchanged life for its own bad blood suggests the threat of racial contamination informing his scientific discourse. But it is not until *The Puerto Rican Peasant* (1887) that he makes the association of this fantastic figure with the "black" body more explicit. In that later work, Atiles repeated that the cause of the anemic condition of the Puerto Rican peasant was hidden in the island's swamps. But now he referred specifically to "a population [that lives] vegetating . . . in marshes and swamps, and which sustains itself with vegetable nourishment and muddy water."[28] This description of a different population that survives the contaminated environment of the swamp was both a subtle reference to the supposed resistance of the "African race" to anemia, and a purposeful interpretation of that resistance.

Atiles conceded that the "white" *jíbaro* was reproducing at a brisk pace, but he also suggested that if anemia continued its unchecked course, a culturally superior "white race" was in danger of being decimated.[29] By the same token, if anemia were left unchecked, the "African race" would flourish. The consequences of this binary, racially determined opposition between resistance and predisposition to anemia suggest a parallel between the "African race" and the figure of the parasitic vampire. The suggestion was that, like a parasitic agent, the "African race" in the colony had something to gain from keeping the environment unhealthy, and from polluting the "mostly white" blood of the Puerto Rican peasant with its own "inferior" blood.

Atiles built upon this racialist theory of disease by describing the predisposition of the peasant woman to hemorrhages during menses and childbirth. He represented a female body whose blood was easily lost.[30] The combination of a female peasant body whose blood was out of control with an invisible parasite whose thirst for blood rid the invaded body of its life was a danger urgent enough in 1887 to recommend the destruction of the invasive "population of parasites." Atiles would modify somewhat this violent recommendation later in his career, but he would not change the racialist spirit in which it was pronounced. In his numerous articles on eugenics, Atiles would stress voluntary sterilization, induced abortion, and marriage counseling as ways to control a population that remained racially problematic in 1914.[31]

Today anemia is understood not as a disease in and of itself, but as a variable condition caused by a number of diseases. From the perspective of modern medical historiography, Atiles was clearly mistaken in his understanding of anemia. A similar "mistake" was made by English doctors with the now nonexistent disease of chlorosis, a disease comparable in form to anemia.[32] Karl Figlio's convincing analysis of this diagnosis, however, helps us to rethink the interpretation of such mistakes as unintentional.[33]

Figlio argues that chlorosis was not a mistake, but a successful ideological construct, which served well two historically circumscribed purposes. It helped to empower an emerging professional group of doctors and it helped to stabilize the middle class to which this group was ascending. Figlio argues that this disease construct preserved a bourgeois social order by displacing social attention off of the harsh working conditions that caused social unrest, and onto a phantasm. Like other recent analyses of medical discourse, Figlio's analysis points to the ideological charge, and to the historical discreteness, of disease constructs like chlorosis.

Anemia worked similarly in the hygienic discourse of the *letrados*. It too empowered an emerging professional class that became the effective manager of an infirm body. But unlike chlorosis, anemia was explicitly related to the poor working conditions of a "white" lower class. This difference might be explained by the fact that, unlike the European doctors, the *letrados* could not directly criticize the powerful class they aspired to replace. Instead, they challenged the local Spanish authorities indirectly, by presenting themselves as the caretakers of a victimized social class. Only an indirect challenge to those local authorities would justify the metropolitan authorities to empower the *letrados*.

But there is another important difference between the *letrado* discourse on anemia and the European discourse on chlorosis. That difference is constituted by the racial component described above. For a professional hygienist, like Atiles, anemia worked to displace the problem, originally perceived by the colonial administration to reside within the "creole" or *criollo* body.

Anemia displaced the difference represented by the "black" body of the newly freed slave farther away from the *letrados'* racial kin, to a discrete disease, and to a body now defined as a wholly different life form. The displacement allowed for a safe transfer of power to the newly sanitized hands of the educated local elites, whose self-serving purpose was to continue to keep difference at bay, away from their own bodies.

Letrado Appropriations

A case could be made that the *letrados* used two related strategies to empower themselves. Medical articles like "Against Miasma" were spaces where figures from popular discourse were first rehearsed, and were then appropriated into "medical" concepts. In these works, Atiles appropriated threatening popular images like the vampire to scare the population into compliance with hygienic discipline and education. The analogous figures of the parasite and miasma were the outcome of these appropriations. A second empowerment strategy by the professional class of *letrados* was the displacement of difference onto two bodies: a "black" body and a peasant woman's body. I have argued that in the hands of the *letrados*, the transition of disease from a metaphorical form to the discrete form of anemia was an index of this displacement of difference away from their own bodies onto the bodies of the members of an "African race." Their construction of an anemic body for the peasant woman was part of the same strategy, whereby the contested space was no longer the male "white" body of the so-called *criollo*, but the peasant woman's body.

Like the figures of the anemic peasant woman and the parasitic vampire, the figure of the midwife also served to empower the *letrado* professional class. As in the case of those figures, gender and race in the midwife were signs of difference, displaced from the *criollo's* body onto a different body.

The midwife was the urban female version of the "black" body of the newly freed slave. She appears prominently in the dystopia "The Flourishing Midwife," a story published anonymously, but whose ironic tone and social content made it plainly the work of Atiles.[34] It is set in a hovel in the capital of Puerto Rico. At the center of the story Atiles places the midwife, a former "black" slave who preys on her past owner, relying on the "white" woman's needlework for sustenance. When the midwife learns that the "white" woman is pregnant, she devises a scheme to abort surreptitiously the fetus, which she sees as a competing parasite.[35] Her scheme is similar to the parasitic vampire's behavior. In the story, the "black" midwife makes the "white" woman drink a variety of virulent potions, which lead to a hemorrhage at the moment of birth. Thus, the midwife performs an exchange of vital fluids similar to the parasite's: she substitutes life (associated by Atiles with the unborn fetus, and with its good "white blood"), for her poisonous brew, and causes the "white" woman's death. Like a vampire, the midwife flourishes at the expense of the life represented by the newborn.

A closer analysis of the midwife's parasitic agency reveals that it is not limited to the deadly exchange of different fluids. The story can also be interpreted as the representation of a deadly appropriation of dated medical knowledge by an astute healer, as is suggested by the story's final scene.[36]

> The midwife, with a pair of rusty scissors, hanging from a belt wrapped tightly around her emaciated figure, cut the umbilical cord, I mean, the **vinse**, which she then proceeded to let waste "much black and evil" blood, and which she later "tied up" with the red colored satin lace, which she had extracted in a bundle from her own breast.[37]

The passage represents the midwife's simulation of an earlier medical discourse and practice. On the one hand, Atiles mocks the midwife's use of a "technical" term to refer to the umbilical cord. The midwife's use of the term *vinse* imitates an overly technical jargon that was the trademark of local medical practitioners, which Atiles had criticized earlier.[38] On the other hand, Atiles criticizes the midwife's unhygienic bloodletting, which ultimately causes the infant's death. Thus, the midwife represents not only racial difference, but also a questionable medical knowledge, which differs from that of the school of hygienists that Atiles represented.[39]

But if Atiles indirectly criticizes an older medicine for lacking common sense, this was clearly not as dangerous a quality as the complete lack of sense that he identified with the medicine of the midwife. Atiles joined other *letrados*, like Brau, when he accused local medical practice of witchcraft. Atiles and Brau decontextualize and ridicule concepts used by local medical practitioners to describe disease. Terms like "air" are highlighted with quotation marks to characterize indigenous medical practice as misguided and ultimately fatal.[40]

Ironically, by accusing local medical practice of witchcraft, both Atiles and Brau rehearsed an ancient strategy of order and rejection already contained within the concept of "air." This strategy has best been described by Mary Douglas, who argues that accusations of witchcraft can work within a community to preserve a social order. She argues that an accusation of an occult and diffuse threat may serve, during a time of social instability, to solve social dilemmas by shifting legitimacy into new patterns.[41] "Air" is an example of a threat used traditionally to discipline, in order to maintain a social order. It is used throughout Spanish America to signify a disease caused by witchcraft. Its form in Mesoamerica is particularly interesting, in the context of its appropriation by *letrados* like Atiles.[42] In a Zapotec community of Mexico the term connotes a life form not altogether different from that of the vampire.

> Whereas *aigre puesto* is inflicted by humans using techniques of black magic, *aigre de hora* is a specialty of various supernatural beings who are dangerous at night and during certain hours of special days of the year. The beings who inflict most *aigre de hora* are known as *brujos de lumbre*, or "fire witches." They are called fire witches because it is their custom to fly through the sky as balls of fire . . . According to some informants, they are spiritual counterparts of actual living people in the town who have the power to transform themselves to this other state of being . . . Collectively, they are spoken of as "the vigilance," which refers to the belief that at night, when the civil authority is not functioning . . . the fire witches go on duty to *vigilar el pueblo*.[43]

By accusing the midwives of witchcraft, Atiles simulates the policing and disciplining functions performed by Zapotecan *aigre*.

But clearly, Atiles wanted to distance himself from such analogies. The reason he mocks the midwife's imitation of medical knowledge is to suggest to his readers that hygienic knowledge was distinct from, and more truthful than, the midwives' simulating practices. By the same token, to distance themselves from the deceptions of both a rarified outdated medicine and a popular medicine, hygienists like Atiles used the educated register of literature. In so doing, they aimed to create, and claim, a cultured middle ground, from which they sought to take hygienic knowledge to the very center of the Puerto Rican family.

And yet, naturalistic stories like "The Flourishing Midwife" and medical articles like "Against Miasma" were also spaces where figures from popular discourse were first rehearsed, then appropriated into "medical" concepts. In these works, Atiles appropriated threatening popular images like the vampire or the witch and traditional devices of order and rejection like the concept of "air," to scare the population into compliance with hygienic discipline and education. The analogous, but clinical, figures of the parasite and miasma were the outcome of these appropriations. Ironically, such appropriating strategies brought the hygienist uncomfortably close to the figure of the simulating midwife mocked by Atiles. The implications of this coincidence would not be lost on the next class of doctors seeking power in the island.

Vampires in the Microscope

Barely a year after the invasion of Puerto Rico in 1898, Dr. Bailey K. Ashford, a lieutenant in the U.S. Army and a representative of a new laboratory medicine already in place among some Puerto Rican medical circles, described the work of hygienists like Atiles as a "fantastic blood picture," and claimed to have discovered the true cause of anemia: "Not climate, nor food, nor bad hygiene, nor malaria, nor anything of that sort, but a worm—an intestinal worm!"[44] Ashford's gaze had drifted away from the "fantastic blood picture" and instead fixed itself on the feces of Puerto Rican peasants to "discover" the *Necator americanus*, or the American version of an Old World hookworm (*Ancylostoma duodenale*), the cause of ancylostomiasis.[45]

The new laboratory discourse, however, appropriated Atiles's network of imagery surrounding the figure of the parasitic vampire, while continuing to use it as a controlling, fear-inducing device. This double appropriation explains why, despite the fact that the *Necator americanus* was a "toothless" version of an Old World hookworm, it was nevertheless initially "seen" by the new laboratory doctors as a parasite that sucked out the blood with its "mouth full of teeth and hooks."[46] Even after this "mistake" was corrected, the figure of the worm was represented well within the network of associations already constructed by the hygienists, in order to scare a population into disciplining itself.

> Daily, to the group of visitors who come to the [Central Anemia Station], a number of worms is shown to them telling them that those parasites come from other individuals diseased like them, inviting them to confirm our claim by looking for worms themselves after the medicine we give them has had its desired effect. After a brief explanation about what constitutes the illness, it is explained to them how it is that these parasites produce small eggs from which emerge the new worms. That these little eggs develop under the shadows of the coffee and plantain trees; in the swamps and in the mud where those small worms swarm. That they attack the naked foot of the peasant, producing boils, and that the repeated apparition of boils causes Anemia. They are warned that the dissemination of the disease is due to the pollution of the ground by the feces, and they are counseled never to deposit them in the open field.[47]

Following the lessons of the *letrados*, the new doctors frightened the peasants by showing them the otherwise invisible agents that caused their critical state. Eerily reminding us of the rhetoric of the colonial discourse with which Brau engaged, the new metropolitan discourse of laboratory medicine reinvested the figure of the peasant with responsibility for his or her diseased state, and, more important, with the signs of difference that the *letrados* had worked so hard to displace. Vagrancy became medicalized into a series of symptoms such as a constitutional weakness or indolence. Moreover, it became intrinsic to the peasants, though this time it came in the form of swarming parasites inside their bodies. If parasites were a metaphor for the "black" body of the members of an "African race," the microscope helped to bring the "white" body of the peasant closer than ever before to that dangerous "race." And yet, in a significant turn from the disciplining practices of the earlier colonial regime, the administrators for the new North American metropolis taught the peasant to discipline him or herself. Self-treatment made possible the alternative of partial political autonomy and self-management, but it was dependent on both the incorporation of the disease and on intermittent outside intervention.[48]

Conclusion

It is clear that in order to offer an alternative to the metropolitan and fatalistic explanation of the colonial situation, *letrados* like Atiles and Brau engaged in a contestatory strategy best described by Gilman and Stepan as cannibalization.[49] The *letrados* successfully answered a European determinist discourse, which by definition placed their own questions on a register that was morally and intellectually inferior to that of the European scientists. Moreover, not only did they succeed in their attempts to undermine the fatalistic conclusions of this discourse, but they did so without directly questioning its validity. This indirect strategy made their empowerment possible. The strategy can be broken down into several parts: First, they incorporated a version of the racially determined theory of degeneration that assuaged the fears of the Spanish administrators. Second, they displaced the threat of difference posed by their own bodies onto a "black" body. This displacement required a different set of strategies, which the *letrados* articulated and practiced: caring for the peasant woman and violently disciplining the members of an "African race."

The cannibalization of the *letrados*, however, did not stop with their appropriation and adjustment of the European scientific discourse. Using strategies and figures belonging to popular discourse and local medical practice, the *letrados* constructed a horror story about vampires and innocent victims that justified their "caring" and disciplining strategies. This fiction was critical to the empowerment and self-definition of a class of *letrados* who struggled against three powerful obstacles: a European scientific model that did not explain their perceived reality, a Spanish administration that did not permit them to advance socially and politically, and a popular local medical practice that offered an obviously smart and attractive alternative to their own practice.

But this fiction was also critical in that it defined a normative state of crisis, or impending rupture, which justified its constant management or vigilance, without demanding repressive measures against the "white" *jíbaro*, nor a radical transformation of the colonial reality of which the *letrados* were themselves a part. This horror story resulted in the legitimation of a modern manager, a doctor, placed at the temporal antipodes of an uncivilized country populated by innocent bodies and vampires. It also resulted in the popularization of the lessons of authority. Vigilance became the central tenet of an autotelic process of self-government and liberal reform, best articulated by the new metropolitan discourse, paradoxically at the cost of the newly acquired autonomy of the *letrados*.[50]

In the endless ebb and flow of these configurations, these images sometimes appear to reveal all too clearly the constructions and exclusions that they seek to conceal. One such image is Oller's painting, another is a photograph of Ashford, who arrived in Puerto Rico as a lieutenant in the U.S. Army during the Spanish-American War. The photograph was taken in 1904, the year in which the Anemia Commission was founded. It appears in Ashford's autobiography (1934), where he uses it to illustrate the careful intervention of laboratory medicine on the body of the Puerto Rican *jíbaro* (fig. 11). The photograph shows Ashford in his laboratory, surrounded by the instruments of his trade (a microscope, a petri dish, and a flask full of liquid), examining the ear of a helpless-looking boy. The caption under the photograph reads, "Dr. Ashford taking a blood specimen from an Anemic Puerto Rican boy," which suggests that the expression of suffering on the

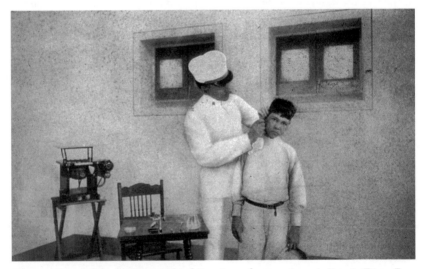

Fig. 11. "Dr. Ashford Taking a Blood Specimen from an Anemic Puerto Rican Boy, 1904." In Bailey K. Ashford, *A Soldier in Science: The Autobiography of Bailey K. Ashford* (New York: William Morrow, 1934), 100.

boy's face is in fact a sign of his illness. While Ashford occupies a central position in the photograph, his ephemeral white uniform, and his face, out of focus, suggest that the microscope, the petri dish, and the face of the boy are the central elements of the composition. The figure of the doctor seems to blend into the background, suggesting the noninterventionist nature of his medical gesture.

Ashford's own account of his practice among the peasants, however, suggests a very different quality to his agency. If one reads this photograph with Ashford's medical report (cited above) of his interactions with the anemic peasants in mind, a different interpretation emerges from the one suggested in the autobiography. Ashford's medical report makes it fairly evident that the boy has just been subjected to a disfiguring intervention.

The presence of a petri dish suggests that, following bacteriological practices, the doctor has been growing a sample of the parasites, in what is referred to as a culture broth. The proximity of the microscope to the petri dish suggests that an examination by the doctor and his patient of its culture broth has just taken place, and that the doctor has explained to the boy that he is the carrier of the worms that he has just seen under the microscope. The frightened expression of the young boy suggests a likely reaction to the doctor's fiction, and explains his voluntary submission to Ashford's intervention. It also suggests the pain felt by the boy subjected to the doctor's invasive practice.

The photograph, then, appears as an ironic record of a vampiric medical practice. It not only shows the doctor painfully extracting blood from the boy for further examination, but it also substitutes the boy's knowledge about himself, and the viewer's interpretation of the boy's expression, with a horror story about the invasion of body snatchers.

The photograph is also an attempt to empower the doctor (his knowledge and his practice) while making him disappear. It is a deceptively self-effacing statement, meant to empower not so much Ashford as the "caring" discourse he represented. In actuality, that discourse remains very much intrusive, and its power comes at the expense of making the boy afraid of himself by turning him into an Other to himself.

Crossing the Boundaries of Madness

CRIMINOLOGY AND FIGURATIVE
LANGUAGE

Introduction

In 1920 the famous Argentinean criminologist, psychologist, philosopher, and essayist José Ingenieros (1877–1925) published a comprehensive history of madness and therapy in Argentina; he narrated the history of both from the new scientific direction taken by Argentinean criminology. He followed an ideological process that required him to describe the earlier scientific paradigms as dated and antiscientific.[1]

> Those of us who have studied mental pathology at the beginnings of the twentieth century, who have understood physiopathological processes with the help of histology, and who have analyzed its causal elements with the help of biochemistry, find it difficult to grasp both the concept of insanity as it was understood a century ago, and the therapeutic procedures that were followed with the intent of curing it.[2]

Ingenieros led a school of criminology in Argentina that began to stray from the path of the earlier school. A review of his scientific works published between 1900 and 1902 shows the core of Ingenieros's differences with earlier criminologists like José María Ramos Mejía (1850–1914). His new school emphasized the importance of the environment over heredity in the etiology of criminal insanity. It also emphasized the technical management of insanity over the classification of the insane.

Despite these differences, however, both schools of criminology believed that the Argentinean nation was undergoing a crisis during the latter half of the nineteenth century, which they both recorded as an increase in the number of cases of insanity in the country. And both schools shared a suspicion of figurative language (religious in the case of Ramos Mejía, and literary in the case of Ingenieros), which they saw as a symptom of the developing crisis, and against which they defined their respective scientific discourses.

An analysis of the differences and similarities between these two schools of criminology will show their use of figurative language to visualize insanity. Examining insanity as a construct will also suggest that they attempted to define the borders of the insane Other, but accomplished something else. In the end, the criminologist interiorized the construct of insanity he deployed, bringing the insane closer to himself than he ever intended.

The Verbally Centered Classic Penal Epistemology

Morphology, in both a scientific and a linguistic sense, was at the heart of the early school of penal science. In so far as morphology is a branch of biology that studies the form and structure of animals and plants, it was the desired materialist end of scientists like Ramos Mejía. His early school of criminal anthropology was concerned with locating within the brain the sources of all intellectual and moral phenomena, and thus was profoundly interested in finding, and accurately describing, the normative pathological brain type: its morphology, its fixed form and structure. In so far as morphology is the system of word-forming elements and processes in a language, it was also a necessary device for the social aims of the early school of criminology: the diagnosis of moral diseases. Vicente Fidel López made this patently clear in his 1878 introduction to Ramos Mejía's *The Neuroses of Famous Men in Argentinean History*, in which he argued that the combination of the science of language and physiology was helpful to the scientist in his incursions into the field of the moral sciences, because it provided a link between the word and organized matter.[3]

The desire to link language and organized matter, however, came not only from the criminologists' incursion into the field of moral sciences, as Fidel López suggests, but also from the historical moment in which the early criminologists found themselves. They found themselves moving away from both an eighteenth-century idealist epistemology, through which disease was understood as a phenomenon separate from the body, with an independent classification system, and a nineteenth-century materialist epistemology, through which disease was understood only in its relation to the body.[4] This historical circumstance, combined with the desire to define ever more concretely the organic boundaries of the mind, led early Argentinean positivists like Domingo F. Sarmiento, López, and Ramos Mejía to attempt to bridge the gap between an abstract, and sometimes transcendental, understanding of disease and a brain that remained for them relatively unmapped.

Paradoxically, in their efforts to move away from a metaphysical understanding of disease, the positivists returned to the close association between language and the body articulated in religious discourse. In Christian dogma divine language is a sign for the body: Christ is referred to as the incarnate word. Likewise, the positivists came to associate divine language with the body. But they did not understand the body as a corporealization of divine language, instead they understood divine language as the external sign of a diseased body. Religious discourse became a place where the scientist went to look for causes, and symptoms, of mental diseases such as obsession. Moreover, religious discourse became a source for metaphors they mined to make mental disease visible to their readers, even as the desired materiality of mental disease continued to escape them. "I firmly believe," Sarmiento wrote,

> in the transmission of moral aptitude through the organs; I believe in the injection of one man's spirit into another by means of the word and through example . . . Perverse men rule by infecting the atmosphere with the vapors of their soul; their vices and defects reproduce themselves . . . and the morals of the civilized, who have preserved the maxims of the great masters through books, monuments, and education, could never have reached its current level of perfection, if a particle of the spirit of Jesus Christ, for example, had not entered into each and every one of us through education and sermons, to improve our moral nature.[5]

In this passage from *Memoirs from the Provinces* (1850), Sarmiento illustrated the material and transcendental crossroads from which were drawn the paradoxical functions of language, as both visualizing device and as disease symptom. On the one hand, Sarmiento drew from religious discourse to build a striking image for genius and virtue. He began the passage with an allusion to the Christian credo and ended it with a reference to the salutary effect of Christ's words. Both references served to remind the reader of the Christian tradition that associated divine language and the body. The reader was reminded that the credo, like dogma, was a set of signs imprinted in memory. But the Christian reader would also remember that in exceptional cases the signs of dogma were imprinted on the body itself, when they took the form of stigmata.[6] Sarmiento compared virtue to stigmata, benign marks on the body that carried the particles of the divine.

On the other hand, Sarmiento also drew from the European theory of miasmatic infection to argue that vice and perversity were the result of propaganda by Argentinean political leaders like Juan Manuel de Rosas.[7] Sarmiento suggested that the printed word was more than a line on a page; words could be like vaporous substances that carried the vices of the perverse. The vicious word, according to Sarmiento, crossed the boundaries of the flesh and seeped into the mind of man like an airborne disease, imprinting itself in his brain according to its nature. Miasma, then, functioned here as a metaphor for diseased language. Miasma stood opposed to the stigmata in that the nature of its imprint was not beneficial. But miasma was like the stigmata in that it too was a metaphor for a language imprinted on the body.

Like Sarmiento, Ramos Mejía also drew from both contemporary scientific and religious discourse to describe a diseased language imprinted on the body.

> The organisms that find themselves in eternal twilight live attracted by two contrary, and equally powerful [physiological and pathological] forces, even though it is more common for the implacable power of pathological attraction to make itself apparent . . . [These organisms] are more receptive to [pathological attraction] because it is usually the case that the soil has been prepared at birth, or even before, in the mother's womb itself, where they receive the seed that imprints on them the incomprehensible sign that predisposes their distinctive cerebral form [to neurosis].[8]

The concept of "pathological attraction" was derived from scientific concepts such as "irritability" in the work of European scientists like G. Tate's *Treatise of Hysteria* (1830).[9] Tate explained the daunting invisibility of hysteria by emphasizing its movement from location to location. He traced its movement from the brain to the spinal column to the womb, turning it, along the way, into a female-coded disease. Like Tate, Ramos Mejía suggested that the invisibility of mental disease was due to its fundamentally peripatetic character, or to its nature as a phenomenon whose defining quality was eternal movement. But unlike Tate, Ramos Mejía used hysteria's etiology to explain neurosis, which was a male-coded disease. He did so by redefining the womb with the help of religious discourse.

In the above passage the womb is not only a contaminated organ but also a contaminating agent of disease, which imprints the brain of the fetus with a neurosis. Ramos Mejía transformed the nature of the womb with references to two principal narratives borrowed from the Bible. On the one hand, Ramos Mejía compared the womb to fallow ground, drawing from the Christian parable told by Saint Matthew the Evangelist of the seed of understanding, which is choked to death by the thorn-covered ground on which it falls. On the other hand, his reference to neurosis as an incomprehensible sign imprinted on the brain of the fetus was an allusion to God's mark in the story of Cain and Abel.[10] Ramos Mejía used both of these biblical stories as visual aids to help the reader picture the womb not so much as a diseased organ (i.e., a passive carrier of disease), but as a contaminating agent (i.e., a material source of disease production).[11] By the same token, these stories helped the reader to see neurosis as the imprint, or language, of the diseased womb on the brain of the fetus.

Unlike Sarmiento, Ramos Mejía associated religious discourse itself with diseased organic matter. In his *Madness in History* (1895), he described Christ as an insane though brilliant man, whose morbid sermons influenced the mind of susceptible medieval men, and whose general influence was devastating for the human race. Thus, while Ramos Mejía used Christian symbols as rhetorical devices to redefine the womb, he also used these symbols as diagnostic devices, as symptoms of the disease that he wanted to illustrate. If he compared the womb to the soil in the Christian parable, and to the hand of God in Genesis, he was comparing it to what were, for him, diseased symbols. In the final analysis the womb was a metaphor for the contaminating nature of divine language itself.

Ramos Mejía's discussion of the *idée fixe* is a poignant example of his portrayal of religious discourse as a diseased language. In his discussion, however, he used to advantage the associations made by religious discourse itself between language and the body.

> The *idée fixe* [a poisoned thorn that is never fastened] is responsible for many great things in the political history of nations. Physiological in its beginning, [the *idée fixe*] changes itself into something pathological through its constant burden on a slightly tempted brain . . . I understand that under these circumstances it is a symptom of a truly diseased brain . . . When an individual is ruled by a persistent, living, and constant passion, which, shall we say, is woven onto a sensibility of abnormal proportions, and onto an ardent imagination, then a mere thought, a simple doubt, is coated with a suspicious fixity, the disease that characterizes the ideas of the mentally ill.[12]

In this passage Ramos Mejía used a string of metaphors and associations literally to coat a diseased brain that showed signs of obsessive behavior, which he considered a symptom of madness. He turned obsession first into a magical thorn, and then into a piece of showy clothing sewn to a morbidly enlarged area of the brain.[13] The thorn was a metaphor for disease. Obsession, like a thorny vine, weaved in and out of the brain, and gradually covered it with an ever more restrictive cloak. The image, however, associated disease and suffering not so much with weaving as with a violent writing on the body. The image conjured the signs of suffering associated with the crown of thorns and the crucifixion of Christ, and made visible to the reader the mate-rial lesions on the brain that Ramos Mejía sought to expose. The passage is an effective redefinition of mysticism as obsession, and an implicit condemna-tion of the divine language of Christian dogma, which is here turned into a set of wounding words imprinted on a weakened brain.

Paradoxically, by turning the womb into a metaphor for a diseased divine language, and its writing (the *idée fixe*, for example) into signs for the suffer-ing it caused, Ramos Mejía turned medical diagnosis into biblical exegesis. His practice became an act of interpretation not unlike that performed by re-ligious scholars. It is thus not surprising that he characterized the signs made by the divine hand (i.e., the invisible lesions of mental illness) as impenetra-ble, and that in what seems like an epiphany, Ramos Mejía read the signs of the crucifixion as a synecdoche for human suffering.

As Sarmiento's simultaneous reading of political propaganda and religious sermons suggested, the acts of interpretation performed by early criminolo-gists like Ramos Mejía were not limited to the words of the Scriptures. Like many of his contemporaries, Ramos Mejía extended the metaphor of a dis-eased language to European literary works that were considered noxious to the Argentinean imagination. This is suggested in a medico-legal report re-garding a doctor whose institutionalization Ramos Mejía recommended to the courts after diagnosing his madness.

> Dr. W. started taking black English drops; first in therapeutic proportions to lessen the pain, later in increased doses to satisfy anomalous appetites, chasing after that pleasurable *euphoria* that takes the opium-eater into one of those *artifi-cial palaces* inside of which crumbled into madness the famous and before cited author of *Confession of an English Opium-Eater,* a typical and classical example of an opium-eater.[14]

It is in biblical exegesis that the reader will find the erased model for Ramos Mejía's intervention in this passage. When Ramos Mejía connected the literary work of popular European authors of the period with noxious, degenerating influences on the mind of prominent Argentines, he was pre-supposing an unmediated connection between the word and the body. This explains why Ramos Mejía believed that Thomas de Quincey's (1788–1859) description of an opium-eater was not only an accurate representation of the madness that overcame Dr. W., but also that De Quincey's work itself was written in a stigmatizing language, a visible and contagious sign of the Euro-pean illness. De Quincey's words were, quite literally for Ramos Mejía, poi-soned English drops.

By turning medical diagnosis into biblical exegesis and literary interpreta-tion, Ramos Mejía not only transformed mental disease into a beautiful object

of analysis, he also amplified the scope of the medical gaze to include all figurative language, making his own discourse vulnerable to a similar diagnosis.
The implications of Ramos Mejía's attempts to turn madness into a visible
object of analysis were understood by José Ingenieros's school of criminology, and the new penal science successfully challenged them.

The Challenge to the Early Penal Science

Ramos Mejía provided Ingenieros with a definition of figurative language as
both a metaphor and a material sign for mental illness, which Ingenieros
used in his own doctoral dissertation. Following Ramos Mejía's musings
about the simulation of health by the insane, Ingenieros became interested
in the simulation of insanity by the criminal in order to avoid incarceration
and severe punishment.[15] Erasing any mention of his mentor, however, Ingenieros described as fortuitous his discovery of the figure of the simulator.

In a passage that stood both as a homage to Ramos Mejía's talent as a
writer and as a self-conscious and blundering attempt to embrace the collective voice of the genre of the scientific paper, Ingenieros told of one night of
study when his eye accidentally wandered to the wall and noticed a dust
ball.[16] After some time, out of the corner of his eye, he noticed a change in its
position. So, being the born clinician that he was, he got up and went to examine this apparently inoffensive piece of debris, and what he found filled
him with surprise.

> At first we thought that it was an optical illusion resulting from a retina fatigued
> by excessive reading; yet, there being neither a real cause for such doubt, nor a
> satisfactory explanation, we chose instead to remove the dust ball from the wall,
> which we then carefully observed. Such is, at any rate, the proper behavior with
> an event that is difficult to explain. And in this case, as it always is, our observation
> was full of rich, profitable lessons. Inside the dust ball we discovered a tube, thick
> and resistant, which would have been impossible to imagine if we had not
> removed the dust ball from the wall; inside this tube there lived a worm, which,
> by means of two extremities attached to its body, fixed itself to the wall and tra-
> versed it, dragging its curious dress along with it. Darwin . . . gave us the answer
> to the puzzle. The useful disguise hid the animal from the dangerous gaze of its
> enemies.[17]

While Ingenieros emphasized Darwin's theory of natural selection, some
credit was due to Ramos Mejía, whose metaphor for the *idée fixe* comes to
mind here. It is true, however, that if Ingenieros appropriated Ramos Mejía's
dress as a metaphor for a diseased language, he also used it in a different way.

In contrast to Ramos Mejía's use of the dress as a metaphor to amplify the lesion, to make it more visible, Ingenieros used the dress as a metaphor for the invisibility of the social disease. The dress was still a sign for the worm's disease, for its simulating nature, but now it also hid the worm, it stood apart from the worm. Figurative language was an external coat that covered the disease, making it invisible even to the gaze of the clinician, and as such it was also separate from the disease, and could be carefully removed from the diseased body by the new figure of the criminologist.

For the new criminologists, figurative language in its various forms (e.g., embellishment, the costume, literariness) was dangerous in the hands of both patients and doctors. If it was a dangerous disguise in the hands of the insane, it was a deceptive tool, a misguiding device, in the hands of the doctor. Insofar as this was true in the case of legal testimony, figurative language should be challenged in court to show the diseased nature of its user. Insofar as this was also true of medical discourse, it should be demystified and excised.

For this reason, the dangerous implications of Ramos Mejía's amplifying strategy, which linked language to disease and literary interpretation to diagnosis, did not escape his contemporaries. In his introduction to *Madness in History,* the naturalized French critic Paul Groussac censured Ramos Mejía's excessive literariness, calling his work a scientific book of chivalry. Restating the warnings suggested by the Brazilian novelist Machado de Assis in his 1882 story "O alienista," Groussac observed that Ramos Mejía's amplifying strategies threatened to institutionalize the whole world and left no one outside to guard it.[18]

Like Groussac, Ingenieros criticized Ramos Mejía's scientific inaccuracy while emphasizing his literary style in his 1915 prologue to *The Neuroses,* an elegiac essay published one year after his mentor's death.

> Ramos Mejía set out to do something very different from what he accomplished. It is evident that he intended to leave for posterity an image of Rosas as "morally insane"; with that goal in mind he accumulated elements for diagnosis without eliminating the equivocal and insignificant. To be fair, he wanted to be impartial, but he included matters of opinion, which resulted in the amplification of the figure of Rosas, which grows from chapter to chapter, from page to page. One cannot but notice a certain kind of authorial pleasure taken from embellishing, with decorative verve, the details of his model.[19]

In this passage, Ingenieros referred to "equivocal and insignificant" elements of diagnosis, to "matters of opinion," suggesting not only the inaccuracy of Ramos Mejía's sources, but also a link between these sources and a discourse, like gossip, that was patently untrustworthy.[20] Moreover, Ingenieros underscored Ramos Mejía's own equivocal use of language, which went beyond diagnosing Juan Manuel de Rosas's illness. Ingenieros suggested that the stature of Rosas as an important Argentinean political figure grew in direct proportion to Ramos Mejía's embellishing diagnosis. The more Ramos Mejía described Rosas's insanity, Ingenieros wrote, the more Rosas's figure grew in importance. Thus, instead of making apparent the danger represented by Rosas's insanity, Ramos Mejía paradoxically made the danger disappear behind the decor of the disease. Rosas, whom Ingenieros regarded as an insane criminal of the most dangerous kind, became, under the embellishing hand of Ramos Mejía, an attractive literary figure constructed with suspicious details and opinions. Ingenieros went so far as to suggest Ramos Mejía's own mild insanity when he wrote that Ramos Mejía actually took pleasure from embellishing the figure of Rosas, a practice that clearly took his scientific work in a direction opposite to the one he intended.

Ingenieros's criticism of figurative language in Ramos Mejía's work can be extended to his views on the morphological nature of the early model of penal science. Ingenieros's criminology removed morphology from the theoretical center of early penal science, which sought to describe a fixed form and structure within what was for him a fundamentally dynamic organ. In other words, Ingenieros was responsible for a shift in the etiology of madness that changed the emphasis from morphology to function. He understood that madness was less the result of endogenous causes such as heredity, than of exogenous causes such as social environment. Unlike his predecessors, Ingenieros argued that, since the causes of morbidity in the brain were not strictly hereditary, the symptoms were not only physiological. This meant that a brain could be ill without showing visible lesions or stigmata.[21] Therefore, the key issue for criminology was not form, but the functional relationships that led to dangerous behavior.[22] He was less interested in the criminal than in his actions, less interested in the brain than in how it interacted not only with the rest of the body, but also with the social environment.

Likewise, the criminologist's gaze moved away from language as a set of diseased signs, and focused on its deceiving function. This meant that the early model of penal science was untrustworthy not only because it was a morphological science, but also because it was rhetorical in nature.[23] It also meant that the new task of the criminologist was to understand this complex mixture of forces acting on the criminal's brain, in order to better advise a court on an effective course of prophylactic or regenerative action, in cases where neither lesions nor criminal activity were clearly in evidence. His new task was carefully to observe and listen to the accused in order to identify, separate, and challenge his lying words, in order to show the court the threat to society underlying them.

The New Criminology and the Metaphor of the Culture Broth

Despite Ingenieros's attempts to rid criminology's discourse of its underpinnings in figurative language, metaphors returned to his own discourse, although albeit in a more "scientific" form. Ingenieros used metaphors drawn from the field of bacteriology to illustrate the implications of the change in the etiology of madness that he was proposing. Such changes meant that social protection or prophylaxis became more important to Ingenieros than the classification, incarceration, and punishment of criminals. Thus, he emphasized methods of cultivation and caring observation, related to prophylaxis, when setting himself apart from the anthropological school of early penal science.[24]

> Those who follow the sociological school have argued that the physio-psychic conditions of the delinquent are complemented by the agency of the environment; those who follow the anthropological school have proven that the environment by itself does not produce delinquents. Both are correct; both are necessary. But far from thinking that they exclude each other reciprocally, they should have seen that neither of them, in isolation, gives a sufficient cause to explain the etiology of crime. Lacassegne contributed an analogy to the debate: the microbe (the delinquent) is not important if it does not find a culture broth (social environment), but, Ferri was right when he underscored that no culture broth can produce microbes through spontaneous generation.[25]

In this passage, Ingenieros represented crime as both a socially acquired disease and as an inherited condition. To do so, Ingenieros borrowed a metaphor from Lacassegne that compared the criminal to a microbe, and his social environment to a culture broth.[26] While the metaphor represented the criminal as an independent life form, it also suggested that its destiny was determined by its environment.[27] According to Ingenieros, the environment, like a culture broth, either nurtured this otherwise harmlessly small life form into a disease of threatening proportions, or cultivated it through vigilance and care for observation purposes.

The caring rapport between the doctor and his patient was further facilitated by a metaphor drawn by Ingenieros from the opposing field of parasitology.[28] For Ingenieros the simulator was like a parasite, an organism with the ability to transform itself into a life form that was different from its parents, but that carried within itself the disease of the parents. It was an insidious agent of illness, which, lacking characteristic, recognizable lesions and physiological traits, had to be carefully studied. The two key concepts of this theory of illness were the intermediate host and the parasitic life cycle, both of which served Ingenieros's purposes well. The paradoxical notion of the parasite suggested that the object of psychiatric interest was both diseased and free from illness, and made it possible for the doctor to get ever closer to his patients.

Thus, instead of using metaphor to amplify the disease, Ingenieros's metaphors reduced the criminal to simple organisms—parasites and bacteria. The key to Ingenieros's use of figurative language lay in his metaphorical reduction of the problem, suggesting its relative simplicity, and the possibility of safely approaching and effectively isolating it. The metaphors emphasized that through caring, clinical, and vigilant observation, the disease could be kept under control.

Ingenieros did not limit his figurative language to metaphors drawn from the emerging scientific disciplines of bacteriology and parasitology. His literary style was also praised countless times since the Nicaraguan poet Rubén Darío first commented on it. In his "intimate confessions" to Máximo Soto Hall, Darío set Ingenieros apart from the majority of scientists, claiming that his style was "polished" and "cultivated," his paragraphs "full and musical, severely wrought, clear and precise."[29] Likewise, and underscoring some of Darío's carefully chosen adjectives, Ricardo Riaño Jauma praised Ingenieros's severity, clarity, and precision, and called him a poet. Riaño Jauma meant by this that Ingenieros was a disciplined observer who kept a tight and salutary reign on his exalted imagination and romantic intuition.[30] Riaño Jauma's emphasis on vision and observation was but a thinly veiled reference to the clinician's discerning eye, and it represented his effort, shared by Ingenieros, to build a discipline based on observable facts, instead of relying on verbal models.

Such attempts were, however, anxious signs of a self-deluding strategy to hide the continuities between different models of knowledge. Not surprisingly, it was at the liminal moment of differentiation from a supposedly transcended model of knowledge that the defining traits of the earlier model reentered the new discourse. This was the case of the return of figurative language to Ingenieros's clinical discourse represented by the costumed worm, the parasite, and the metaphor of the microbe in its culture broth.

Ingenieros's Approximation to the Diseased Other

Ingenieros used his most spirited figurative language in his description of another liminal space. This time, however, it was the space between the new medical discourse and the Other it sought to observe and regenerate.

> Surrounded by beautiful and wide gardens irrigated by a gentle brook which the sun turns golden with its lukewarm rays, and which in turn makes mysteriously

powerful forces burst out of their buds in a *lustful efflorescence of corollas*, there emerges, slender and beautiful, the body of a building made to house those who commit crimes, victims of their own psychic morbidity. And, surrounded by the perfume of flowers, by the abundant light, by the vastness of the horizon encompassed by the gaze of the visitor, and by the echoes of the music performed by a band of gentle madmen, which modulates its harmonies nearby, the idea that this is the house of the human beast, a mixture of madness and perversity, does not come to one's mind, as it did in the past.[31]

In this description of the hospice of Las Mercedes, Ingenieros deployed an elaborate metaphorical system in order to paradoxically show the needlessness of such decorative devices. But first, drawing from sources that included Ramos Mejía's germ-soil metaphor, Ingenieros represented the hospice as both the center of a series of concentric circles irrigated by a fertile liquid, and as a natural body emerging in the midst of plants. He argued that the hospice's appearance both as a nurturing broth, and as a budding plant, countered the fear felt by the visitors who associated the dangerously insane to human beasts. Thus, through the combined use of both metaphors, by turning the space for insanity into a beautiful and nurturing private garden, the visitor (and the doctor) could draw ever closer to the figure of a cultured, music loving, humanized insanity.

An intriguing and complementary tier of signification emerges, however, when the reader considers that Ingenieros put both images in italics. To highlight the rhetorical devices at the moment when they are deployed suggests Ingenieros's ironic use of the metaphors to underscore the artificiality of the space he described. The irony in the passage hinted a cautionary, paradoxical message to its readers. It suggested that while the insane may be changed from a seed to a microbe to a concert pianist, the change was always figurative, and could always be reversed.

For Ingenieros the insane remained dangerous and only seemed harmless, and, more important, the treatment remained coercive and only seemed humane. If he highlighted the elements of a metaphorical system that seemed to change the function of mental institutions from discipline to caring vigilance, it was to suggest to the reader that, like him, Ingenieros recognized the compensatory metaphors in his own discourse, and like the reader, he was not fooled by them. By highlighting them he suggested that the metaphors he himself deployed were ultimately decorative in nature, and thus secondary to the defensive task at hand: protecting society from potentially dangerous beasts.

But his defensive use of irony also suggests Ingenieros's anxiety at his increasing approximation to the insane, which followed not only from his humanization of the patient, but also from an awareness of his own status as a son of Italian immigrants, a literal pool of insane criminals according to the new school of penal science. Ingenieros's approximation to the insane Other was increased by a sense of his own alterity, developed during his trip to Europe. In 1905 Ingenieros traveled to Rome as the Argentine representative to the Fifth Congress of Psychology, with commissions both to study the European penal systems and to serve as foreign correspondent for the Argentine newspaper *La Nación*. Ingenieros traveled to the land of his predecessors in a return to what Sergio Bagú described in his biography as Ingenieros's intellectual or virtual origin.[32]

Ingenieros, however, clearly felt a tension within himself when migrating to the perceived scientific metropolis. In a letter he wrote from Europe to the Argentinean novelist Roberto Payró, describing the nostalgia and tension he was suffering, Ingenieros returned to a version of the figure of the parasitic simulator, only this time he used it to describe himself.

> I am like a strange butterfly; time goes by, my youth fades, my wings develop, I try to fly, but the light neither intoxicates me nor blinds me. The metamorphosis does not affect my feelings; I live and I think, as if I were a butterfly, but I preserve intact the attachment to the chrysalis. In the new sheath I guard jealously the perfume of the old communions.[33]

The beautiful butterfly seems here to be at the antipodes of the diseased worm inside its dust ball. And yet, Ingenieros presented himself in the passage as a parasitic life form: as both different and the same from "the old." He compared himself to a butterfly still attached to its cocoon, inside of which Ingenieros guarded his attachment to his past. The chrysalis that Ingenieros could not abandon stood here for the discourse of the early penal criminology, whose figurative language continued to haunt Ingenieros, even as he attempted to disassociate himself from it by keeping up with the latest European discoveries.

But Ingenieros's use of the metaphor of the sheath can also be diagnosed with his interpretation of figurative language in mind. A member of the new school of Criminology headed by Ingenieros would argue that the sheath worked here as a disguise to fool the enemy, much like the dust-ball surrounding the worm. This reading would suggest that the sheath served Ingenieros to guard his less cherished aspects from the inquiring gaze of his European counterparts. From this perspective, Ingenieros is shown to imitate the insane's defensive and simulating behavior.

The *Travel Journal* Ingenieros wrote during that year-and-a-half-long trip contains moments of awareness of his difference from his virtual origin. During such moments Ingenieros unwittingly came closer to the bodies against whom he leveled his own disciplining practices. Writings like the above make the reader appreciate the degree to which Ingenieros had interiorized the figural archetypes for insanity that he had himself constructed together with his mentor Ramos Mejía.

Conclusion

The debates between intellectuals in what would seem to be divided and specialized territories like the fields of the classical penal system and the new school of criminology, are but autotelic, self-referential simulacra of dialogue and negotiation, which confirmed, with their purported independence, a normative state of crisis for the Argentinean nation. As such the function of the different metaphorical systems used by all sides of these debates was always compensatory. Metaphors like the thorny vine were used to naturalize and universalize an invisible crisis, making it visible as well as configuring it as a nonthreatening object of knowledge. Similarly, metaphors like the microbe in the culture broth shifted the focus away from a universalization of the crisis (without undermining that effort) to a technical administration of it.

But figurative language was also more than a compensatory device used by Ramos Mejía and Ingenieros to construct a crisis they would then set out to manage. Figurative language was also at the very center of what constituted dangerous alterity, or insanity, for both scientists. Thus, they both built a scientific discourse to distance themselves from that which they considered the insane Other to be. In the process, however, they turned themselves into versions of the Other they had constructed. Ramos Mejía became a metaphysician, while Ingenieros became a poet and a simulator.

5

The Crisis of Memory

REMEMBERING MACHINES AND SELF-GOVERNMENT

> Memory . . . is an abyss inhabited by representations which invade the writer's present, cut him off from nature, separate him from himself. Not surprisingly Flaubert . . . describes the abyss of memory as a catacomb inhabited by an interminable series of corpses which constitute a history inhabiting the present of the writer—a present which the writer is forbidden to inhabit.
>
> —Eugenio Donato, *The Ruins of Memory*

Introduction

Perhaps inspired by Nietzsche's thoughts on breeding an animal with the right to make promises, Eugenio Donato argues that the enlightened and scientific attempt at knowing ourselves, at making ourselves knowable and understandable to ourselves, leads to a necessary violence.[1] This violence (which he calls an epistemology of crisis) reduces and disciplines an intersubjective, infinite, and timeless becoming, separating it into discrete units such as subject and object, language and nature, mind and body. Memory is the instrument of this Romantic violence that separates the Self from becoming, and produces a sustained series of funereal metaphors for the Self, of which the Flaubertian catacomb is but one.

Written at the end of the nineteenth century, *The Water Hole* by Manuel Zeno Gandía and *After-Dinner Conversation* by José Asunción Silva both incorporate and attempt to transcend this European epistemology of crisis that dates back to the seventeenth century. Indeed, both novels stand as familiar techniques of memory, helping their imagined subjects to "fabulate" and discipline their past in such a way as to give it a recognizable, dispassionate, ideal form. Both novels, however, are also allegories of the simultaneous invasion of the Self, and of its present, by the very crisis that their techniques are meant to regiment and govern. In fact, the novels are reminders of the paradox that results when the Self unwittingly inscribes into its fabric, or folds its fabric into, the crisis or structural abyss that gives it the psychological depth and the memory necessary for self-knowledge and self-government.

In this chapter I will argue that each novel constitutes its subjects through a different mnemonic process, but I will also argue that these two processes are but separate stages of a two-stage compound remembering machine. First, images are produced in the mind through a process compared to the simple machine of the *camera obscura*, an instrument dating to antiquity, consisting of a darkened chamber or box into which light is admitted through a hole to produce an image of external objects. Then, the mind gathers, orders, and projects these "palpitating images" onto a film that moves rhythmically through the mind's eye. This projection produces the illusion of a linear thread of events, and results in what appears to be a stable interiority.[2]

Memory, in these novels, is a self-preservation device; however, it is a device that paradoxically produces funereal images for the Self. Like the magic lantern in *A Remembrance of Things Past*, memory in these novels is a therapeutic instrument whose effect is not necessarily stabilizing.[3] While memory first isolates, becoming into discrete units, these units are as shifting and confused as gusts of wind. They are like the sleeping poses of the Proustian body, which is in the process of becoming conscious by assuming successive positions. Moreover, while memory makes these units more coherent by giving them movement, the connection necessary to make them move further challenges the discretness of each unit. Thus, while both *The Water Hole* and *After-Dinner Conversation* begin as mnemonic attempts at self-government, they end with the image of degenerating bodies falling into a temporal and spatial abyss. They both end with prefigurations of the Proustian composite memory of ribs, knees, and shoulderblades whirling round inside a dark tomb.[4]

The sustained production of these funereal metaphors radicalizes the questions raised in the novels about the process of self-formation and self-government. Thus, while both novels fall short of what Donato calls an "active forgetfulness" of the past, necessary for a definitive break with a self-centered model of authority and government, they nevertheless prepare the way for willful writers who will demand to actively forget the hollowed shape of our subjectivity, and the hallowed ground of our mind's I.

Learning to Read the Body

Graduated with a degree from the Central Faculty of Medicine in Madrid, Spain, in 1875, and after residency work in France, Manuel Zeno Gandía practiced medicine in Puerto Rico for over twenty years. A hygienist, Zeno Gandía worked for the Department of Maritime Health in Ponce (the port city at the southern part of the island). In 1887 he wrote a manual on the hygiene of infancy, which earned him membership to the Imperial Pediatric Society of Moscow.[5]

He called that manual "a spelling book of health,"[6] and meant it to be perused regularly by its female readers, for recreation and education. It taught mothers how best to take care of their infants, in the absence of constant medical supervision. Its content was presented as scientific knowledge, the very opposite of the erroneous and superstitious knowledge of a midwife. By regularly reading the manual the mother's instinctive love for her infant would turn into a reasoned and intelligent love, Zeno Gandía argued. The manual claimed to make "the book of nature" intelligible to her. It made it possible to *read* the body of her child for symptoms of an otherwise invisible disease. In this way the manual could prevent the death of the infant, which it described as a loss that deeply wounded the heart of parents.[7]

In the introduction to that work, Zeno Gandía used the metaphor that would be the centerpiece of his later novel *The Water Hole*. He warned that it was criminal for parents, and specifically for the mother, to fail in their responsibility to redeem their children both physically and morally. He compared this criminal act to a fall into a contaminated water hole or *charca pestilente*. To prevent this metaphorical fall into a liquid void, Zeno Gandía represented the child as a network of visible signs (including physiognomy, mimicry, attitude, robustness, sounds), whose health depended on the professional use of various technical devices (i.e., medical charts, clinical case histories, measurements from the *pesaniños*). These devices both minutely regulated the distance between the infant's body and the body of the woman breast-feeding it, and closely monitored the infant's gradual changes in weight and height. They both managed and constructed a body as a calculable network of lines crisscrossing both time and space. Zeno Gandía hoped that, armed with such a battery of visualizing technical and scientific devices, his vigilant readers would help prevent the liquidation of the delicate individual, on whom depended the health of the nation. With these devices he transformed the infant's body into a grammar: a portable, two-dimensional network of signs.

The manual also turned the female body into a similar network of readable signs. In order to preserve the well-being of the child, it fragmented the movement of the female body into distinct positions, and measured the normative distances between it and the body of the infant during breast-feeding or sleep. The manual further fragmented the female body into its constitutive exterior and interior parts, offering normative dimensions for the size of the nipple, and measuring the normative density of its milk. Like other nineteenth-century medical works, the manual also traced emotion, nervousness, and hysteria back to the reproductive organs in the female body, and turned these so-called moral qualities into organically visible signs.

Perhaps Zeno Gandía should have called the manual the spelling book of health and disease, for in it he also taught women to read disease into their own bodies. Comparing the child to a delicate plant and the mother to the soil, the manual naturalized this general association. By paying close attention to the production and management of breast milk, it turned this association into a particular one between disease and the mother's liquids, and collapsed the female body and the body of illness into one comprehensible whole.[8] It warned women against their own bodies, implicitly comparing them to water holes into which the delicate infant might sink. By teaching women to read their own bodies and the bodies of their infants in this way, the manual also taught them to associate the female body with the origin of the infant's disease.

Reading the manual amounted to providing the necessary critical distance from the female body to prevent the infant's death. By turning the bodies of infant and mother, and their points of interaction, into a network of readable signs, the manual prepared its reader for self-analysis. Reading and rereading questions like "what is an inappropriate level of irritability in a prospective mother?"; "what is the normative size of her nipples?"; and "what is the normative density of her breast milk?" the female readers would become distanced and critical about their own bodies and psychological makeup. By providing comparative tables to so-called normal bodies, and describing so-called normal psychological profiles, the manual gave mothers abstract guidelines to regulate their own conduct. Following the measurements, tables, fragments, signs, collected in the manual, the reader was to examine both the body of her infant and her own body to determine whether to nurse her child, to give birth to a second, or even to have a first.

This act of critical distancing, however, had its organic limits. Despite its claim to train the reader in self-analysis, the manual was also clear about the fact that the highest authority remained always with the doctor. The hygiene of infancy was described as an elemental branch of the tree of medicine, easy to grasp by mothers already predisposed by instinct to spend time with their children. But the doctor's superior knowledge should always be consulted, it warned, in the search for the best hygienic advice.

Reading the manual was a *subjecting* act in both senses of the word. On the one hand, to read the manual was either to subject female figures (the midwife or the mother) to the superior authority of masculine figures (the doctor), or to subject the female body to the superior force of the disease that the manual aimed to prevent. In its turn, the manual dominated disease by dominating the female body: by transforming the body into a network of organic signs, and then associating those signs with disease.

Through this double act of domination, the manual further created a subject, or a self-critical consciousness. The manual separated a consciousness from the female body by making it aware of its own disease. It further turned this consciousness into an ever vigilant observer of its own diseased body, by threatening it with the responsibility for the death of its own children. As the editors of the manual succinctly put it, *"The Hygiene of Infancy . . .* familiarizes mothers with what they ought to know, and at the same time it lets responsibility fall on those who are guilty of abandoning their children."[9] The manual thus constructed a consciousness through a metaphorical wounding process. Through the sustained reading of the manual's inscriptions of disease in her body, culminating in the threat to her heart (an organ considered synonymous with the feminine body), the reader separated herself from her body. This separation guaranteed that the subjectivity that emerged from reading the manual was *critical* in both senses of the word: it was self-aware and it was in crisis.

Images from a Magic Lantern

In his manual, Zeno Gandía separated the diseased female body from an educated, self-critical subjectivity to prevent the fall of the body into a contaminated water hole. In his novel by that title, he showed the female mind undifferentiated from this body of water, presented it in its naturally liquid state. He compared the female mind both to the disordered flow of images reflected on a river and to the disordered flow of images in a magic lantern show.[10] The show was a private screening for a male audience now held responsible for taking the necessary steps to bring the diseased female body under control.

The beginning of the novel finds Silvina, an anemic peasant woman, looking from the top of a hill at the roaring river flowing down below her feet. While Silvina appears to look at the natural panorama, in fact she looks inside her own self. She is impassive to the "poetic exterior" and thinks only about her inner world: Ciro, the object of her desire, old memories, and recent impressions. Compared to an inanimate statue that cannot see the "living" images in front of it, she is obsessed with artificial memory images made of light.[11] These artificial but "palpitating" images are implicitly compared to the landscape reflected on the river water flowing at the bottom of the hill. Her inner vision is like a recording of light images reflected on the river's surface. Her past is parallel to the images of the Puerto Rican countryside reflected on the river. Thus, while the passage distinguishes between the personal and the national, between an interior and an exterior world, between artificial and natural images, it also collapses them into the single metaphor of silent celluloid film: moving images of landscape and memory, combining space and time.[12]

Silvina's contemplative pose turns deadly by the end of the novel, when she literally collapses into the river in an epileptic fit brought about by an onslaught of memories.[13] The scene begins with a description of the river as a lymphatic liquid, suggesting a resemblance to Silvina, whose anemic condition brings about the hysterical crisis. The image of a pale fluid containing white blood cells like blood plasma suggests that the river carries the fatal blood disease contaminating Silvina's body. But the passage also transforms the biological metaphor into the scene of an artificial show. The lymphatic liquid is also described as the carrier of celluloid-like scenes: palpitating images that record the suffering of the Puerto Rican people at its riverbanks. Like the river's bitter synthesis of collective pain, Silvina is also the screen of a silent film of wounding memories.

As in the novel's opening scene, Silvina looks at these images and is transported to a parallel emotional world of memories. She remembers a series of violent scenes that together make up her life, as well as the plot of the novel. The dramatic show ends when Silvina feels a bitter and strange sensation. Surrounded by the "veil of dusk," she loses consciousness, sees a fiery band of light, and is struck by "voltaic" spasms that throw her down the ravine and into the river. The veil, light, and electricity combine to turn Silvina's death into a visual scene: the end sequence of a picture show.

The Water Hole's opening and closing scenes associate the female mind with hysteria and anemia. In its natural state, the passages suggest, the female mind flows with the deadly disorder of a river, producing a chaotic flow of images like a magic lantern. The disorder in the flow of images and in the flow of liquids suggests the dangerous nature of a body whose flow of blood is difficult to contain or control. The passages show the female mind and body in its normative anemic state, destined to a violent fall.

These suggestions become explicit when the novel's doctor makes the connection between Silvina's hysteric and epileptic fits and her diseased body. Dr. Pintado examines Silvina, and finds that her anemic condition is so serious as to be incurable. Despite his inability to cure her, or perhaps because of it, the doctor turns his examination into a visual image for a few select friends he meets later for dinner and conversation. In his narrative, Dr. Pintado metaphorically dissects Silvina's body to show the disease inside of it.[14] He cuts away at her body to bring out her pounding heart for his dinner companions to see. The heart he discovers lying within Silvina's anemic body is a parasite. It simulates the ebb and flow of life, but is in fact responsible for the living death of its innocent host, whose earthen color is described, in turn, as a simulation of life. Pintado's image emphasizes the dissimulating nature of Silvina's disease. The disease is inscribed as a parasitic heart that poses as a normal heart. The doctor suggests that Silvina's body and her organs are but dissimulating screens behind which the disease hides.

But Silvina's body is also a screen in another sense. Her body is a screen on which Dr. Pintado projects her disease both to amuse and to educate his male audience: Esteban, the region's priest, and Juan del Salto, wealthy landowner and the novel's male protagonist. The doctor's allegory suggests a task for the emerging triumvirate of social medicine, the church, and the wealthy private citizen. They must first assemble the disordered images that haunt Silvina into an intelligible network of signs, a map, not unlike Zeno Gandía's own novel. They must then project this map onto the screen of the body, and finally they must cut the body where the disease is found to extract it.

The novel's opening scene emerges then as the preliminary step necessary to carry out the hunt for Silvina's disease. It begins to draw the intelligible map. It inscribes the female mind as a disordered flow of liquid cell-like images in need of order, cutting Silvina's mind into distinct pieces. Dr. Pintado's narrative, on the other hand, rehearses the final moments of the hunt by cutting open the screen/body and extracting a treasure from inside it. The scene produces Silvina's anemic heart, which, we are told, induces the attack of epileptic hysteria, and is responsible for Silvina's disordered memories.

The beginning of the novel inscribes Silvina as a disordered Self, but the doctor finds the cause of Silvina's disordered memories inside her. The doctor uncovers a treasure that has been covered for him to find. Silvina's dissimulating heart, described as a screen for her disease, is also a screen for disease images projected by the narrator of the novel onto her body. The discovery of the dissimulating heart is then, itself, a screen hiding the original act of inscription from the reader. If the novel's ending reminds the reader of the act of inscription, it also suggests that Silvina's stream of consciousness is the cause of the novel's labyrinthine plot. The diseased female mind then becomes a screen for the agency of the novel's author.

Mnemotechniques and Self-Analysis

Between the beginning and the end scenes, we find Juan del Salto engaged in a similar hunt, but this time he is shown applying the doctor's therapeutic advice to himself, in an attempt at self-government. He orders his own memories into a thread of historical events in order to cure himself of his melancholy. The exercise, however, proves surprising, as it leads him to a neurasthenic attack. Like Nietzsche's dreamer who mistakes the sensation produced by a distant cannon shot for the cause of the cannon shot, del Salto mistakes the dis-ease produced by his mnemotechniques for the cause of the neurasthenic attack.[15]

Del Salto is a self-made man and the wealthy owner of a productive coffee plantation. Like Silvina, however, he is haunted by moments of melancholy, which he faces by "giving himself over" to the bitter memories, and dear recollections of an internal world.[16] Every night, he performs the mnemonic ritual that seems to be an antidote to melancholy.

As in the earlier passages with Silvina, the personal exercise is extended to the history of the Caribbean island, taking del Salto from the island's racially impoverished beginnings to its present abandonment by the colonial authorities. But if in the earlier passages the suffering of the countryside is reflected by Silvina's memories in an accumulating chaos of flowing images, del Salto combines his past with the past of the island in a single thread of historically ordered events. The combination of the protagonist's memory with the island's nature and history is compared to a "living" book, whose pages are analogous but not quite identical to the "palpitating" images of the magic lantern.

Paradoxically, the therapeutic reading of this book ends with a "reflexive neuropathy" that splits the protagonist into conflicting epicurean and idealistic tendencies. The psychological split prevents him either from solving his personal problems or from finding a solution to the degenerate condition of the Puerto Rican population.[17] It leaves del Salto as inert as a statue.[18]

But his inertness conveys the very opposite of Silvina's. Del Salto is not obsessed by the strong inner passions that make Silvina oblivious to the external world. Del Salto is shown in his dark study, illuminated by an oil lamp, sitting at his desk, his head in his hands, thinking. He is thinking so hard that his mind separates from his body. In fact, the mnemonic ritual is the coup de grace that establishes del Salto's intellectual mastery over his passions.

Thus, following traditional gender-coded oppositions, the passage highlights the difference between the novel's principal characters. If Silvina is a slave to her unruly passions, del Salto is a master over his body. If Silvina is governed by her body's repeated attacks of memory images, del Salto governs himself through an active use of memory, or mnemotechniques. If Silvina decomposes into a disfigured, bloody, formless mass of broken bones, del Salto decorporealizes into a series of personal and national memories to become an ethereal consciousness.

Del Salto's act of reading brings attention to the manual's proposal of self-government through a subjecting self-analysis. In order to understand his own life, del Salto slices his life into separate memory bits. Like an editor cutting and rearranging pieces of a movie, he chooses the critical moments to assemble his story: his family's financial catastrophe, the death of his parents, the death of his wife. The Self then emerges as the assembly of these critical moments into a meaningful narrative, not unlike the novel, which claims to emerge from an assembly of Silvina's memories. Moreover, the repetition of the critical scenes has a numbing and distancing effect on del Salto, which results in an ethereal consciousness that appears to separate itself from a body in pain.

Unlike the manual, however, the novel also dramatizes the fragmentation on which this constitution of the Self depends. Once begun, the cutting or editing process intensifies, until it separates both characters into their gender-coded constitutive parts: red and white blood cells in Silvina's case, a schizoid personality in Juan del Salto's. In either case, the violent fragmentation necessary for analysis or self-analysis brings the characters to a paralyzing and deadly crisis.

Moreover, the cutting process does not end with their disease, and is not limited to their individual bodies. Their disassembled selves are followed by a procession of sickly, pale beings, first observed by the medical gaze of the narrator, and then dissected at an autopsy in an attempt by the novel's doctors to explain and give meaning to their slow and inevitable deaths. But again, the "scalpel of analysis" leaves behind only a labyrinth of displaced and wounded entrails, a collection of heterogeneous pieces extracted from a network of cavities empty of meaning.[19]

The Water Hole, then, suggests that the Naturalist act of self-analysis, or the act of reading the grammar of the body, is a necessary act for self-government. It inscribes both the need and the means for self-government. By wounding the body and then "finding" the disease inside of it, the novel stimulates the reader's consciousness first into existence and then into action. Indeed, the fatal nature of the disease is a prerequisite for the apparition of consciousness. The incurable dis-ease that emerges from self-analysis is consciousness itself, the Self necessary for self-government. This is why the novel insists that one read the human document, or see the film of memory images, despite the fact that both acts lead to the dis-ease that the novel tries to diagnose and control. Reading the grammar of the body is tantamount to dissecting it, to digging the holes of consciousness into it, to hollowing the mind out. Rather than "reveal" the memories of anemic or liquidated selves, the violent process imprints consciousness and then screens it with organic metaphors. Consciousness, like disease, emerges from this figurative process as a buried organic cavity, as a network of rhizomes or tubercular parasites, both impossible and necessary to govern.[20]

The Protective Folds of Memory

On May 5, 1894, José Asunción Silva, a prominent member of Colombian society, recognized as a poet by his peers but economically bankrupt, was given the commission of secretary to the Colombian delegation in Caracas, Venezuela. On that same date, Silva finished "The Umbrella of Father León," a short piece of fiction and a biting allegory of what he called "our time of transition."[21]

In this short prose piece, Silva describes the operations of memory. Zeno Gandía compares the untrained memory to the disordered flow of visual images of a magic lantern; in this work, Silva similarly describes memory as an artificial light show that transforms bodies into bright colors and dark shadows. But if Zeno Gandía represents memory in its natural state as a wounding process that leads to a future crisis, Silva represents it as a protective process that transforms, preserves, and safely transports corrupt bodies from the past to the future.

"The Umbrella of Father León" was written as a prologue to a compilation of articles by leading Colombian intellectuals on Father León Caicedo. Clearly commissioned as a collection meant to show respect for Father León, its prologue nevertheless begins with an unflattering portrait. Silva locates the portrait in the present, and he insists that the description is inspired by the actual sight of Father León. Silva emphasizes the strange nature of the figure, its mixture of pure lines with grotesque details, its regular profile with crazed green eyes, its noble head on a diminutive body. He also highlights two details from his attire: a monocle made for a cyclopean eye, and the incredible umbrellas that protect him from rainy days.

This initial description of Father León is followed by a second one, imagined from a future point in time. In the future, Silva writes, not only will Father León be dead, but it will be impossible to look to the present in search of the vulgarized or beautified memories of him. Instead, the sound of his name, rather than the sight of his person, will "evoke" another image, as precise and suggestive as the earlier one.

The "new" image appears under the artificial light of an electric street lamp. While it seems very different from the first image, the new one actually condenses and reassembles the lens and the umbrellas of the earlier one. The cyclopean monocle and the incredible collection of umbrellas reappear in the form of a goblin's dress and possessions. The body of the apparition is completely covered by an umbrella-like black cloak and a hat with an uncommonly wide brim. It carries a single colossal red umbrella and a lantern with green reflecting lenses.

Silva then associates this fantastic memory image with the past of the capital city. He describes the figure returning from a visit to two old women who have treated Father León to the "innocent" pleasures of "sleepy" Santafé (the eighteenth-century name for the capital): the smell of papaws, the art of Gregorio Vásquez, the sweet taste of dessert and tobacco, the fantastic and apocalyptic stories from its colonial past.

The image is then suddenly displaced by a third. The black goblin is transformed into a black *coupé* pulled by a team of red horses headed toward Bogota's new opera house. The carriage is the property of the corrupt minister of a city where fantastic tales have been replaced by clandestine emissions of currency. The minister's profile is only glimpsed by the viewer, who is easily distracted by the minister's wife, of fin de siècle fame, neurasthenic and sparkling with diamonds. If the former composite of Father León displays the "innocence" of the colonial past, the "new" image suggests the pleasures, corruption, and scandals of a cosmopolitan city.

As between the first and second images, the apparent differences between the second and third images hide remarkable similarities. Lit by the same bolt of electric light, the third image is also a composite of Father León's personal belongings. It turns the protective folds of the red umbrella into the red and black carriage that transports the minister safely to the opera house. It transforms the bright lights surrounding the dark goblin into the distracting brilliance of the carriage and of the jewels worn by the minister's wife. Just as Father León's body is protected from the rain by the folds of his gigantic red umbrella, the red horses, black *coupé*, and brilliant diamonds of the third image hide the minister from sight.

Memory, according to Silva, works like the umbrella of Father León. It protects his dead body, and the lost past associated with it, under its idealized folds. But memory also operates like the electric light shining above the images. It is a device analogous to the transporter beams of science fiction fantasy. It carries the idealized traces of a lost past into the future, even as it simultaneously transforms the portrait of a dead priest into the living profile of the corrupt minister.

This last insight into the workings of memory turns the newly appointed secretary of the Colombian delegation in Caracas into a shrewd political analyst. By "times of transition" he does not seem to mean the transition to a different future. Rather, his portrait suggests that the apparently new economic order of Colombia's emerging capitalist economy is but the old religious order transported and transformed. The connection between minister and priest further suggests that the fantastic nature of the economic manipulations by the corrupt liberal administration that appoints him is not altogether different from the fantastic and apocalyptic tales that ruled Santafé in the past.[22]

The role played by memory in Silva's political analysis couldn't be more different from the use of mnemotechniques in Zeno Gandía's work. For the Puerto Rican doctor, the act of reading manuals and novels is tantamount to learning self-government by rote; it stands opposite to the hysteric magic lantern show. To read is to form the mind, to inscribe consciousness, to memorize, and to discipline. Following Anatole France, Silva instead compares books to "works of sorcery" from which emerge images and spirits that transform the Self, and to "magical apparati" that transport the Self amid those images of the past and supernatural shadows.[23] Reading, for Silva, is identical to a mnemonic process that he implicitly compares to a magic lantern show. Like memory, he suggests, reading creates the mind out of the body, gives the body psychological depth, transforms the traces of the corrupt body into the protective folds of memory, which hide and transport something other than a self-critical consciousness through time. Just what is transported in this fashion is further developed in Silva's 1895 novel, *After-Dinner Conversation*.

The Scene of Reading and the Camera Obscura

Reading is also a central topic of *After-Dinner Conversation*. The illuminated book that appears in the novel's opening passage is a diary whose pages are reproduced in the novel, and make up its bulk. Indeed, the after-dinner conversation of the title refers to a public reading of that diary by the novel's protagonist, José Fernández, who also happens to be the diary's author. In the first entry of that diary, Fernández distinguishes his reading of a second diary (the *Journal of a Young Artist* [1889] by Marie Bashkirtseff) from those of Max Nordau and Maurice Barrés. Using a metaphor that is also the model for the mind in Nordau's theory of consciousness, Fernández compares the work of both writers to the photographic plates of a *camera obscura*.

According to the theory of consciousness developed in Nordau's *Degeneration* (1892), the Natural Object or the External World creates consciousness, the brain—in short, interiority itself—through a photographic process modelled after the *camera obscura*. According to Nordau, the External World makes imprints on the body. When the External World comes into contact with the body, it wounds the body at the cellular level, and produces a network of internal cavities that become nerve cells, nerve ducts, brain cells, and the brain proper.[24] Once formed, these cavities produce and preserve a memory image of the original stimulus or disturbance. Described by Nordau as both the embodiment and as the slave of the External World, consciousness is a hollowness that reproduces the images of that world.[25] The body and the mind, as imagined by Nordau, are networks of *camera obscuras*, formed by the very imprints they are meant to reproduce. Thus, it is not surprising that Nordau compares the "lowest degree of art" to the pictures of a *camera obscura*, because for him consciousness in its most primitive form operates like that device.[26]

According to Nordau, the degenerate consciousness is unaware of its origin and master, and suffers from hallucinations as a result. A degenerate consciousness is a malfunctioning *camera obscura* that cannot grasp the mastery and unity of Nature. Either it thinks that memory images are external stimuli (Ego-Mania), or it thinks that external stimuli are memory images (Mysticism). Either way, it does not understand the difference between the stimulus and the memory image, it does not "read" the imprint left by the External World back to its origin, it remains forever apart from its true origin. This misreading and resulting separation from the Natural World is the cause of dis-ease.

Nordau's theory of consciousness is used by Dr. Rivington, a character in Silva's novel, to diagnose Fernández's neurasthenic hallucinations. Fernández's hallucinations are confirmed when he is shown a painting of a woman that bears a striking resemblance to Helena, a young woman he saw only once and has dreamt about ever since. While the painting is clearly too old to be the portrait of Helena, Fernández is nevertheless ready to swear that Helena was the painting's subject. So uncanny is the apparent identity that Fernández recognizes her white robe, the white flowers, and even the Latin verse written on the painting, as parts of his memory of her. These hallucinatory episodes become more intense as the year ends, and have a clearly degenerative effect on Fernández. The year's end brings with it a full-blown neurasthenic attack that puts him in a comalike state. Fernández remains unconscious for a number of days, even weeks, only to begin anew what appears to be a yearly cycle. Aiming to cure himself of these nervous attacks, the protagonist decides to consult Dr. Rivington, the author of a work titled "Natural Causes of Supernatural Apparitions."

During the consultation, Dr. Rivington explains that memory is like a *camera obscura*. First, the natural world is transformed into an image by light admitted through the camera's eye. This image is then projected and recorded onto a negative plate, which is saved in the camera's dark room. Finally, a circumstance stimulates the selection of one of these plates, and brings the negative out of the dark and into the light, producing a positive image of the past event.[27] Rivington uses this mechanistic theory of consciousness to diagnose Fernández's neurasthenic symptoms. To identify the painting as a painting of Helena, he suggests, is to invert the temporal order of succession, the order of cause and effect produced by the mnemonic process, and paralleled in the operation of the *camera obscura*. Indeed, the doctor believes that the painting is not of Helena, and instead argues that Helena (or at least the Helena that Fernández thinks he remembers) is actually a memory image, a phantasm, of the painting. The doctor supposes that Fernández saw the painting as a child and received an impression of it that stayed with him inside his mind. Then, when Fernández met Helena, the analogy between her physiognomy and the physiognomy of the subject of the painting stimulated this negative image to emerge from its hiding place. This stimulus then resulted in a false negative, which combined Helena, the painting, and the writing on the painting, into one memory image.[28] The Latin verse that Fernández associates with Helena is evidence of the false nature of the memory image. To read a verse in the memory image of Helena is to have a false memory of her.

Following Nordau's therapeutic process, Rivington believes that Fernández must first realize that the Helena he is dreaming about is not the original Helena, but a memory image of a painting. Second, he must understand that by confusing this memory image with the original, Fernández keeps himself apart from Helena, and from the Natural World that Helena represents. In other words, Fernández must perform a therapeutic act of demystification. He must read the Latin verse back to the painting, not to Helena. Finally, Rivington believes, Fernández must look for the original Helena to cure himself. He suggests that by finding Helena and marrying her, Fernández will cure himself of his hallucinations.

For Rivington and Nordau, subjectivity is created through a hollowing-out process. The process is identical to the subjecting process described in *The Hygiene of Infancy* and in *The Water Hole* by Zeno Gandía. Both Max Nordau and Rivington compare the mind to a dark cavity, or a *camera obscura*, which not only receives impressions from the outside world, but is created through those impressions. The mind is a deposit for memory images, according to Nordau and Rivington. The accumulating plates or imprints add volume to the mind, making it expand with time. The imprints then create a temporal chain of stored memory images that take up space inside the mind giving it literal, and figurative, depth.

Similar to Juan del Salto's mnemotechniques, exposing these imprints and reading them back to the first impression are exercises in self-government and self-analysis. To govern itself, the subject needs to know what it is and what it is not; it must know the chain of memory images that constitute it and must identify the false associations. Self-government and well-being are the promised result of this act of self-reading.

The exercise, however, also has a price. It creates a Self whose consciousness collapses into the body of disease. As in *The Water Hole*, this act of self-reading reveals an original violence. Well-being paradoxically implies reading the imprints back to an original wound, to an original dis-ease. Rather than curing disease, the mnemotechnique exposes the disease at the point of origin of consciousness. But the doctors are ready to pay this price because to make consciousness coextensive with disease is also to conform it to a set of known variables and values.[29] This conformity makes the critical consciousness manageable. By inscribing consciousness as disease, Zeno Gandía, Nordau, and Rivington create a manageable Self in a permanent state of crisis, in permanent need of self-government and self-analysis. But they also turn the state of well-being and normality into an ideal state that must be attained at all costs, as dis-ease invades from all directions.

Screen Memories and the Layers of the Mind

Fernández's efforts to seek advice from Dr. Rivington and to give direction to his life suggest that Silva remains interested in stable, manageable subjectivities. But the subjectivity that emerges from his novel also suggests that he might not be as ready to pay the price of Rivington's cure. Subjectivity, for Silva, is not the result of a physiological hollowing-out process. Instead, it surfaces from a process that seems to be the very opposite of the act of self-analysis as it is practiced by Zeno Gandía, Nordau, and Rivington. It emerges as a dressing, as the result of a self-conscious, figurative process that covers (rather than inscribes) the wounded body with layers of metaphorical screens. At the beginning of that process, the reader still finds a wounded body, a memory trace. But now, the trace is also transported to the end of the process, and rather than contain consciousness, it hides and protects something both deeper and more superficial than consciousness.

Dissatisfied with Nordau's and Rivington's photographic and taxonomic readings, Silva's protagonist claims to read differently. Light falls on Bashkirtseff's open journal, filtered through Japanese crepe, as Fernández "reads" the diary through the *Spiritual Exercises* of Saint Ignatius Loyola (1491–1556).[30] His act of reading is actually a mnemonic "composition of the place" following Loyola.[31] Closing his eyes, he "composes" Bashkirtseff's room, and then imagines her in a pose that significantly mimics his own.[32]

Sitting at a desk in her room, surrounded by her favorite books, the lukewarm light of her lamp shining through her full head of brown hair, Bashkirtseff remembers her day as a sustained series of creative bouts with the reality of her fatal illness.[33] She is dying of tuberculosis, but her exercise transforms the corporeal disease into a symbol that she does not recognize.

"Men of science" describe her tuberculosis earlier in the passage as a growth of tubers, invading and devouring the inside of her body, crawling under its skin, hiding behind her delicate breast. Maurice Barrés's "negative" extracts the disease and transforms it into the tubercular form of flowers adorning Bashkirtseff: a bouquet of anemones and mimosas covering her bodice.[34] She takes the transformation process further by erasing the memory of her disease with the character of Ophelia. She "drags in" Ophelia's pale corpse and blond head crowned with flowers by playing Beethoven.[35] Her music playing creates a "consoling divine phantasm" that transforms Bashkirtseff's disease into the mortuary wreath crowning Ophelia's corpse.

The scene is also an out-of-body experience. It separates Bashkirtseff from her body to the point that she does not recognize Ophelia's corpse as a prefiguration of her own death. The separation and defamiliarization depend on the same layering process. Her dying body is screened by the image of Ophelia's corpse, just as her tuberculosis is screened by Ophelia's madness and crown of flowers. But the screening process not only substitutes her body with Ophelia's, it also seems to transform her body into a consciousness. As in Zeno Gandía's manual, the passage appears to represent the formation of a consciousness through education and discipline.[36] Moreover, her fantasies, described as "potent, rich, solid," are the combined fantasies "of ten men" and erase her "delicate feminine hands." Like del Salto's nightly decorporealization, the apparent abjection of the female body produces a masculine consciousness: scenes mastered by literary "superior men" and transcendental masculine subjects.[37]

But Bashkirtseff's production of screen memories and burial of her feminine body also suggest an investment in, and a protection from, the organic process of the disease. Ophelia's scene suggests that simply to oppose the obstinate divine compositions of an artistic soul to the symptoms of an equally adamant diseased body will not be a sufficient cure. The recurring symptoms of tuberculosis fix the disease back in its original corporeal place. But they are also the pretext that gives shape to that scene. Indeed, the creative layers under which she hides her body in Ophelia's death scene are the remnants of Bashkirtseff's own liquidated body. The stings and chills that she feels on her breast are the raw material for the screen memory that shields her breast from those same bodily symptoms. Thus, her tuberculosis also provides the traces that are arranged into the therapeutic screen memory. The screen memory transforms the signs of Bashkirtseff's liquidation, her chills and stings, into the water and the crown of a dramatic scene. The memory image transforms, preserves, and represents her tuberculosis.

Unlike Zeno Gandía's critical consciousness, however, Bashkirtseff's remains blind to the meaning of the distancing images produced by the exercise. It is, in fact, this very blindness that the exercise seems aimed to produce. And indeed, the systematic process of symbolic displacement into dramatic scenes, which preserves and transforms the remains of her body, appears to be effective and therapeutic. The exercise distracts Bashkirtseff, who forgets both herself and her disease. Together with drops of opium, the exercise proves calming, and puts her to sleep. When she wakes up the next day, and looks at her rosy cheeks and her smiling brown eyes in the mirror, she is oblivious to her condition.

Like a doctor dressing a wound, she dresses her disease with layers of symbols, screening it, covering it up, transforming it, rather than exposing it. This subjecting process is different from the one described by Nordau and Rivington. They suggest a process that depends on sense perception, or on tracing a series of memory images or "negatives" back to the original physiological event responsible for consciousness and disease. For Nordau and Rivington, subjectivity emerges as the accumulation of those "negatives," or steps, back to or away from an original wounded body (consciousness). Modeled after Loyola's exercises, Fernández's subjecting process is very different. It makes room for, and hides, a third intimate register different both from the inside of the intellect, and from the outside of sense perception. Subjectivity emerges instead as the accumulation of screen memories, or dramatic scenes, made with the organic traces of the original physiological event, but covering and displacing it.

Screening the Unconscious

Julia Kristeva in *La révolte intime* finds in Loyola's *Spiritual Exercises* a preparation for what she calls the Freudian turn.[38] She convincingly argues that, despite Loyola's aim to submit sensuality to reason through his spiritual exercises, he presupposes a "coalescence of the sensorial and the spiritual." It is this coalescence that Loyola seeks to visualize in his exercises: "an interior vision" that is neither perception nor thought, that is image, or in Kristeva's terms, that is the "imaginary."[39] According to Kristeva, Loyola's images preserve the bodily senses in dramatic scenes, despite his own efforts to separate language from the body. These scenes, suggests Kristeva, are the pre-texts for Freud's unconscious.[40]

Silva's metaphor of memory as a screen is drawn from Loyola's dramatic scenes. For Silva, memory projects rather than imprints an image. Memory blends body and language, rather than writing language on the body. Not surprisingly, the same metaphor reappears in Freud's early psychoanalytic writings. In his 1899 essay "Screen Memories," Freud looks to Greek myth for his metaphors, comparing memories to a veil that clothes someone with beauty.[41] Like Zeno Gandía and Nordau, Freud believes that the experiences of childhood leave traces in the depths of our mind.[42] According to Freud, however, these ineradicable traces are *screened*, in both senses of the word: they are screened by memories in the sense that they are transformed and hidden by them, and they are screened in the sense that memories are made from these traumas on organic tissue, which makes trauma visible to the psychoanalyst. The screen memory, then, is both a cover for the unconscious, and it is the unconscious. Like the folds of a veil covering and revealing the features of a face, the unconscious is both the inside and the outside of the organic traces.

According to Freud, subjectivity is not the end result of a process that begins with the inscription of consciousness. It is not a stable chain of memory images leading back to the past, to the moment when consciousness was originally inscribed. Like the unconscious, subjectivity is instead the result of an unstable creative process full of tension. It is the result of a pastiche of memories, of a series of idealizations and transformations, which occur after a traumatic event. According to the young Freud, the mind is made of two contradictory principles. The first tries to imprint memory, while the second resists that impression, transforming and erasing it. Subjectivity, then, is not reducible to, and cannot be brought back to, an original consciousness. Unlike Nordau, who believed that consciousness can lead us back to its original trace, Freud believed that the "raw" state of the dead tissue at the origin of the subject remained forever unknown to it.

Freud's subjectification involves a process that Nikolas Rose has provocatively compared to an invagination of an outside. Rather than think of the unconscious, or the subject, as an interiority, Freud imagines and constructs it as an organic fold, "not unlike aspects of the body that we think of as part of its interiority—the digestive track, the lungs."[43] Its folds "incorporate without totalizing, internalize without unifying, collect together discontinuously in the form of pleats making surfaces, spaces, flows, and relations."[44] But, despite its challenge to the previous process of subjectification, like Zeno Gandía and Nordau, Freud still constructs subjectivities. That is, he still collects, incorporates, in short, creates what Julia Kristeva calls an intimacy.

If self-analysis as practiced by Zeno Gandía and Nordau produces a subject that amounts to a cavity filled with the empty tubers of consciousness, Freud's psychoanalysis produces a subject made of folds of beautified dead tissue. Indeed, the veil is a screen for the dead body. It is significant that in the article on screen memories, Freud's patient emphasizes the importance of a scar on his face, to which the analyst pointedly does not return. Instead, Freud moves the reader's attention away from that scar with his dramatic reading of the memory scenes. He turns his patient's attention to his bodily drives (to his hunger and sexuality), when the scar would seem to point in the opposite direction, to a dead body without drives. Psychoanalysis helps, then, in the necessary act of self-delusion, or screening, that infolds a liquidated body into a subject. If memory screens (hides and reveals) the unconscious, psychoanalysis similarly screens the death at the origin and at the end of its notion of subjectivity.

Screening Death

Curiously, another meaning for the title of Silva's novel (*De sobremesa*, in Spanish) is a piece of cloth that protects and hides the empty space under a table. The diary inside the novel is the result of just such a veiling process as is made patently clear by Fernández, who, by his own account, transforms the symptoms of his strange neurosis into a literary work.[45] The government of the Self, in the novel, depends on a similar covering of emptiness, dramatized by the novel's beginning and end.

After making the obligatory references to Baudelarian artificial stimulants (tea, coffee, alcohol), the beginning of the novel associates their hallucinatory effect with a mysterious portfolio at its center. Light shines through a patterned screen and casts shadows on a crimson book that stands out from the surrounding exotic bric-a-brac. The novel's closing passage is a subtle variation on this opening scene, associating similar shadow play with the same portfolio at center stage. The passage (and the novel) ends with the comparison between the luminous play and the fantastic dance of a fairy tale, suggesting a magical effect produced by the images projected on the book.[46] Like color forced through a silkscreen to paint, rather than to imprint, an image on a surface, the light that shines through the screen creates a similar density that turns into a fairy tale.

The framing passages alert the reader to the fact that he is "in literature."[47] Like the passages of Zeno Gandía's novel, these are part of a *mise-en-scène*, or a set piece, that dramatizes a light show. The opening play of light and shadow images highlights the artificiality, the drama, and the theatricality of that scene. The images further suggest that the novel is a "magic device," and that reading it will conjure both images from the past and supernatural shadows. Like Loyola's spiritual exercise, the play of light and shadow highlights a necessary and creative displacement. The clutter of the scene (the smoke, the fragile china cups, the blood-colored cover of the portfolio, the atoms of gold dancing inside a transparent liquor from Dantzig), protects, hides, and reveals the violent and traumatic losses of Silva's life. In particular, the scene is a screen for the emblematic loss of the novel's original, which was famously lost to the sea, in the shipwreck of the *L'Amerique*. The scene also foreshadows Silva's suicide, one possible result of a subjecting process based on similar screenings of death.

Conclusion

Finished within one year of each other, *The Water Hole* (1894) and *After-Dinner Conversation* (1895) appear during a crisis of authority in Spanish

America, when, in the words of Sylvia Molloy, "a received order is slowly replaced by a produced order."[48] They were written at moments of intensified challenge to centralist, and received, political regimes both in Colombia and Puerto Rico, whose monumental authoritarian subjects would be slowly and gradually folded into networks of individual subjectivities.[49] The modern liberal regimes that followed from these challenges to an authoritarian overseer were based on the production and implementation of individual techniques of self-administration. Both novels are early models of such subjecting techniques, specifically of mnemotechniques.[50]

While involved in similar subjecting exercises, Zeno Gandía and Silva produce different subjects. If Zeno Gandía's work creates a critical subjectivity by turning consciousness against its own body, Silva describes the unconscious process of idealization that hides the body from consciousness. If Zeno Gandía suggests that self-government depends on self-analysis, Silva finds that self-government depends instead on psychoanalysis. These different subjecting processes construct different metaphors for themselves. If Zeno Gandía and Nordau privilege imprinting processes and their devices, such as the book, the manual, and the *camera obscura*, Silva and Freud instead prefer screening processes and their devices, such as the fairy tale and the magic lantern.

But such neat differences hide important similarities, which I have attempted to underscore in this chapter. Zeno Gandía's and Nordau's subjecting process is a model for self-government that depends on the metaphor of the mind as a *camera obscura*. On the one hand, they urge their readers to apply to consciousness the simplicity of a *camera obscura*, the transparency of its internal image. On the other, they leave readers to assemble on their own all the parts of the *camera obscura*, until they make the consciousness visible. To assemble the machine is to mimic its very operation by giving consciousness a visible, knowable form. To assemble consciousness is also to do violence to the Self. What is at stake in this subjecting process is the inscription, cutting, editing, carving, and hollowing out of an interior space for consciousness, and the further widening and deepening of its outlines by repeating the process. Not surprisingly the subject unwittingly assembles itself in such a way as to meet the necessary condition to return to the infinite whole out of which it originally came; it surfaces as a hallowed corpse.

Silva's early version of psychoanalysis is a screen for a similarly violent process. If Zeno Gandía's work first inscribes and then hides consciousness, Silva's work reveals and hides the unconscious with those very layers. Like the reader of Zeno Gandía's works, Silva's reader will emerge as a subject in the very act of assembling the magic lantern. What is at stake in this assembly is not only an original wound, or even the repetition of that wounding process. Instead, what is at stake is the displacement, transformation, and revelation of an original corporeal trauma into an unrecognizable form. Silva's subject emerges as a funerary urn containing and revering its own relics.

Conclusion

There are a thousand paths that have never yet been trodden, a thousand forms of health and hidden islands of life. Man and man's earth are still unexhausted and undiscovered.
　　　　　　　　　　　　—Friedrich Nietzsche, *Thus Spoke Zarathustra*

Crisis is a decisive moment in a scientific, literary, and political sense. A body, a text, or a political or economic state are equally liable to be in the grip of crisis. To be a subject of crisis is for the body, the text, or the state to be momentarily dominated by the uncertainty, indecision, and strain of the critical state. It is my claim in this book, however, that to be the subject of crisis can also mean something quite different: it can also mean to be made of crisis. To be the subject of crisis is to have crisis as the essential substance, as the constitutive material. It means that a liquid state defined by its transience is the normative condition of a body, a text, or a political or economic state.

Subjects of Crisis: Race and Gender as Disease in Latin America is about the different ways in which intellectual elites in Latin America come to believe, and make their readers believe, that Latin America and its population are in a state of constant crisis. Intellectual elites writing at the end of the nineteenth and the beginning of the twentieth centuries in Latin America saw two principal kinds of difference as a threat to the stability of their societies: sexual and racial difference. To neutralize this perceived threat, the intellectual culture constructed a widespread metaphor for Latin America as a subject of crisis. Described by its intellectual culture as a geographically daunting region, a racially handicapped people, a hysterical female body, or an unbalanced psychological subject, Latin America appeared to be in a normative state of crisis. Described in this way, the region appeared to call for the management, or government, of difference by the very members of the culture that first perceived the problem. Conversely, the object of government would be the bodies, populations, and collectivities identified both as different and as in crisis.

I have here described scientific, literary, and political writings about crisis, which, together or in opposition, visualize and diagnose forms of crisis such as madness, anemia, degeneration, revolution, or colonialism. These writings also trace these crises back to a body. The body that originates crisis is marked in these discourses as of another race or gender, but, most important, it is marked as a natural and physical body. Its matter is fact, its matter is truth according to these discourses. The government of crisis is the production of that material body, of its truth.

Despite the claims of the authorities articulating these medical, literary, or political discourses, the body of the Other is not a matter of fact. It is, instead, a discursive artifact that is specific to a time and place.[1] It is a construct whose physicality is produced and is at stake. The process that produces that body, however, is heterogeneous and changes over time. It involves both debate within distinct discourses and dialogue between different knowledges. The body that emerges from these debates and dialogues is not the result of a carefully orchestrated conspiracy, and it is not a fixed artifact. Like the discourses giving it shape, it is constantly changing and shifting. And yet, despite its heterogeneity, the body is claimed by all of these discourses as a physical object of knowledge.

To make the body physical is not just to lay the groundwork necessary to govern the body. It is to govern the body. It is to turn it into a visible network of lines and depths. It is to turn it into a landscape, or into a map, where conflict, tension, and disorder have coordinates. Thus, to govern the body is not just to control, subdue, discipline, and normalize it. To govern the body is to know the body; it is to have a perspective on the body that makes it visible. By the same token, to govern the body is also to have a perspective on the heterogeneous devices, techniques, and practices available to us to produce "more intelligent, wise, happy, virtuous, healthy, productive, docile, enterprising, fulfilled, self-esteeming, empowered" bodies.[2]

The price of this way of neutralizing the perceived threat posed by difference, of this way of governing, is a reduction in human potential, hope, and promise. It restricts the ability to question or criticize the process of perception; it limits the understanding of knowledge; it confines the creative act; it leads to repetitions and clichés. Most important, perhaps, this reduction, and the resulting practices of government, lead to suffering.

The suffering is due, in part, to the relationship between the perceived threat and the metaphor produced: their identity. One mirrors the other, and they are both matters of fact. Indeed, the metaphor confirms the inability to escape the perceived threat. The threat of difference can be managed, but it is unquestionable. Moreover, the endemic nature of the threat of difference inevitably affects the society at large. It even determines the shape of the soul and the psychological makeup of the cultural elite itself. The intellectual elite's strategy, then, does not contain, but rather spreads the perceived problem. It leads to an apocalyptic perspective from which disease is seen as rampant, and total catastrophe is feared to be just around the corner.

Insofar as a government is a perspective gained both on the body and on the devices that produce and govern the body, it is also an event that has a history. In this book, I have also traced the history of a specific shift in government first diagnosed by Michel Foucault: the shift from an authoritarian, central, direct form of government to a liberal, decentralized, indirect one. Such a shift also brings about an alteration in the perspective of the governing gaze, from the body of an Other to the Self. It also brings about a modification in the interest of the techniques of government from physiology to psychology.

It has been pointed out that to articulate the shift to modern government in such a way is to (re)present the problem that cultural critics like Foucault are trying to diagnose. In other words, it is to visualize government, its techniques, and the body in terms that suggest a nostalgia for the authoritarian, direct, and masculine government that these cultural critics appear to indict.[3] Surely, more attention must be paid to the violent forms government takes even after the turn described by Foucault. But to argue that to diagnose the shift is to feel nostalgic for the past is to miss the promise offered by the changing patterns of government, and by the uncertainties that produce them.

This book has traced the transformation in Latin America from disciplinarian to pastoral forms of government.[4] Through an articulation of different discourses (scientific, literary, and political) I have described a shift from a notion of government based on producing sexually and racially different bodies with critical structures to a confessional form of government that incorporates patterns of that very crisis. Despite the shift, the result remains the same: a governed subject. The notion of a governed subject does not constitute a problem in and of itself; however, the specific forms of government and self-government apparently chosen by the subject in these works are a problem.

One of the implications of the analysis carried out in this book is that the subject does not so much choose a form of government, as a government chooses a form of subject, but it seems equally true that forms of government unravel themselves through their own logic. By inscribing or folding crisis into the body or into the self, governments manage the body or the self only temporarily, until their techniques and technologies are proven to be ineffective by the very nature of the produced subject.

Even though *Subjects of Crisis* takes as its object of analysis the work of "diagnositicians of sickness" writing at the end of the nineteenth and the beginning of the twentieth centuries in Latin America, its principal argument speaks also to the present in the United States. A similarly perceived threat by sexual and racial difference has produced similar metaphors: the balkanization of the United States, the degeneration of American values, the corrosion of the country's moral fiber, and the country's moral malaise. The similar collapse of the figurative and material registers into one dead certainty has led to the uncommon preoccupation with endemic diseases that appear to affect collectivities with sexual and racial markers. "Diseases" such as anorexia, AIDS, PMS, or sickle-cell anemia emerge as biological certainties, when they are unmistakably marked by culture and ideology at the very point of their "discovery."

The state of crisis then easily spreads to education, to the family, to the government, and to the economy. Indeed, crisis seems so pervasive in today's culture that it reaches the highest and most exclusive of social and political circles. During one week late in 1998, two related statements bore witness to this perceived state of widespread crisis. On October 3, referring to the banking crisis in Japan, the president of the United States proposed "contingent finance to help countries ward off global financial contagion."[5] Three days later, referring to the Monica Lewinsky scandal, a member of the House Judiciary Committee considering initiating an impeachment inquiry against President Clinton commented, "we are witnessing nothing less than the symptoms of a cancer on the American Presidency."[6] The "cancer" was a veiled reference to a woman preoccupying Washington, and a hackneyed gender-coded metaphor for the threat posed by sexual difference; the "contagion" veils a well-worn reference to the Orient and its "unhealthy" racial difference.

Widespread metaphors of disease such as these belie striking similarities in our way of visualizing and perceiving racial and sexual difference. Conversely, they expose a similar way of "seeing" the nation, the economy, and the presidency, as a delicate, fragile body that must be protected. Latter-day diagnosticians of sickness, we offer a "diagnosis" of, and we suggest a "prognosis" for, sexual and racial difference. We think that racial and sexual difference are threats to the healthy body. The implication is that, like a disease, racial and sexual difference must be studied, managed, and eventually "cured."

Such strategies tend to backfire. They inevitably lead to the perception of a state of widespread vulnerability, precariousness, contamination, and erosion. This imagined normative state of crisis *sometimes* leads to similarly violent responses to maintain a stability continuously under siege, to contain the damage already done. The normative state of crisis, however, *always* leads to a defensive, suspicious, punitive, and self-disciplining attitude that prevents generosity and creative leaps of interpretation—in short, the best within us—which, under other circumstances, would help us imagine and live in a better future.

It seems better to step back from the certainty of the crisis and to study the uncertainty that pervades the acts of perception and creation that give crisis its present forms. Does difference, be it sexual, racial, cultural, or otherwise, begin and end at a definite point, as so much political or social discourse would have us believe? Is there a measurable, physical, even genetic, point where white (for example) separates from black? Is that point devoid of meaning, that is, of the meaning we choose, or sometimes are forced, to give it? What would be the implications of admitting the depth of our uncertainty? In *Subjects of Crisis*, I attempt to speak from that uncertain ground. I try to make strange, or less familiar, the connection between the metaphor and the threat, and thus expose its artificiality. What is at stake is not the transparency of a natural reality, but rather the possibility of a more generous interpretation. By critically examining our most familiar territory, our commonplaces, our clichés, all of which give us a sense of security, we create the conditions that might transform our future. By changing our past, we make a different future possible.

Notes

Introduction (pp. 1–12)

The translation of all texts is my own, unless otherwise specified.

1. Stabb, 12–33. Stabb offers convincing evidence from the work of a number of essayists from the turn of the century. These writers include the Argentinians Agustín Alvarez, Manuel Ugarte, Carlos O. Bunge, and José Ingenieros, the Venezuelan César Zumeta, the Bolivian Alcides Arguedas, and the Peruvian Francisco García Calderón. Stabb further extends his argument to the Mexican positivists under the regime of Porfirio Díaz.
2. Ibid., 12–13, 219. Stabb's psychological argument here owes much to Samuel Ramos, "Psychoanalysis of the Mexican," in *Profile of Man and Culture in Mexico,* published in 1933 and 1934.
3. Ibid., 32.
4. Ibid., 12.
5. Ibid.
6. Ibid., 34 n.
7. S. Ramos, 86.
8. Vasconcelos, 148.
9. Cook, 201–16.
10. Rose, *Inventing*.
11. My understanding of the sustained explanatory force, or the continuous authorizing function, of positivist and humanist analysis owes much to Foucault's concept of the "author function." Foucault, "What Is an Author?" 148.
12. In every society the production of discourse is at once controlled, selected, organized, and redistributed by a certain number of procedures whose role is to ward off its powers and dangers, to gain mastery over its chance events, to evade its ponderous, formidable materiality. In a society like ours, the procedures of exclusion are well known. Foucault, "The Order of Discourse," 52.
13. From this perspective, my work is also different from the fascinating work done in a related area of cultural studies, which nonetheless presupposes a strict difference between biological (or medical) events and cultural events. Emily Martin's *The Woman in the Body* is an example of this type of cultural study, which is in turn aligned with recent medical anthropology, and in particular with the school within that discipline that distinguishes between "illness" and "disease" (see Arthur Kleinman's *The Illness Narratives,* for example). Such distinctions are called into question in my work. Indeed, the centrality of "discourse" is

meant to imply that medical perception, scientific observation, and literature are part and parcel of a network, which must not be studied and should not be described as the distinct and different parts of a coherent whole.

14. Foucault, *Birth,* 109.
15. Ibid., 4.
16. Ibid., 195.
17. Mel Tapper convincingly argues that "race and ethnicity are always discoursive categories." My analysis of anemia here owes much to Tapper's claim that diseases like sickling are discoursive practices of anthropology and medical science, and are used for the purposes of distinguishing between two races. Tapper, "Interrogating Bodies," 178.
18. Rama, *La ciudad.*
19. Oliver, *Family Values.*
20. Rose, *Inventing.*
21. Nietzsche, *Genealogy,* 87.

1. Walking Backward to the Future (pp. 16–45)

1. *Carguero* literally means carrier. Another name for them was *sillero,* which is a reference to the chair strapped to the carrier's back where the traveler was fastened. According to most travel narratives, it was a profession mainly held by so-called Indians from the high plateaux, although some travelers pointed out that this was not always the case.
2. In his analysis of the figure of the *carguero,* Taussig vividly paraphrases Charles Cochrane's description of this role reversal:

   Extremely galling was [the traveler's] dependence on the *sillero* and porters, who held their masters at their mercy. They were notorious for deserting and would always loiter, complaining of strange fevers and rheumatism of the neck. From these heights of suffering the end to Cochrane's journey was dramatic. Around noon his *sillero* turned suddenly to climb down an almost perpendicular precipice backwards. While Cochrane faced a 2,000-foot drop, his carrier descended, clinging to tree roots and calming his terrified passenger. (Taussig, 302)

3. The book was first published in French with the title *Vues des cordilleres et monuments des peuples indigenes de l'Amerique.* My references are to Helen Maria Williams's translation: *Researches Concerning the Institutions and Monuments of the Ancient Inhabitants of America, with Descriptions and Views of the Most Striking Scenes in the Cordilleras* (London: Longman, 1814).
4. I borrow the term from Mary Louis Pratt's discussion of travel narratives in South America in her fascinating *Imperial Eyes.*
5. Examples of passages describing the *carguero* can be found in Charles Stuart Cochrane's *Journal of a Residence and Travels in Colombia during the years of 1823 and 1824,* Carl August Gosselman's *Travel through Colombia 1825–1826,* John Potter Hamilton's *Travels through the Interior Provinces of Colombia* (1827), Charles Empson's *Narratives of South America* (1836), Isaac Holton's *New Granada* (1857). For later examples of the economic adventurer's experience of the *carguero* see *Trip to the New Granada 1869* by Charles Saffray, and

Equinoctial America by André Edouard. They can both be found in Eduardo Latorre Acevedo's *Fabulous Colombia's Geography*.

6. I borrow the term *letrado* from Angel Rama's *La ciudad letrada*. It is a reference to an elite class of educated or lettered men responsible for shaping and governing the different Spanish American republics after the revolutionary wars.

7. Ramón Torres provides another striking example in "Old Way of Travel through the Quindío," published in *Museo de cuadros de costumbres*.

8. Taussig, 298.

9. Ibid., 299. Ramón Torres's travel account is a defensive response to the European criticism of this mode of transportation.

10. Santiago Pérez (1830–1900) went on to become president of the United States of Colombia between 1874 and 1876. The commission was headed by the Italian colonel and geographer Agustín Codazzi and was charged by the radical liberal government of José Hilario López (1850–1854) with drawing a general map of the republic and of all of its provinces. It was active for a period of nine years, until Codazzi's death of malaria in 1859. During that time, nine different mapping expeditions were organized and carried out. Pérez joined the commission after the second expedition, and followed Agustín Codazzi until the sixth expedition.

Codazzi was accompanied by Manuel Ancízar during the first two expeditions. Before that, Ancízar had been a diplomat working for the moderate conservative administration of Tomás Mosquera (1845–1849) who was responsible for recruiting Codazzi. The founder and director of the newspaper *El Neogranadino (The New Granadian)*, Ancízar was made the official chronicler of the commission, and was charged with "describing the customs, the races in which the population is divided, the ancient monuments and natural curiosities, and all other circumstances worthy of mention" (quoted in Caballero, 149). Ancízar would later publish his travel accounts in two volumes titled *Peregrinación de Alpha por las provincias del norte de Nueva Granada 1850–51*.

After the first expedition it was decided that the commission would profit from the help of an illustrator and a botanist. The illustrators changed over the course of nine years. While there were three official ones (Carmelo Fernández, Henry Price, and Manuel María Paz), there were also a number of unofficial illustrators who worked in between the recruitment of the authorized ones. Many of the watercolors have been reassembled and reproduced by Jaime Ardila and Camilo Lleras in the beautiful book *Batalla contra el olvido*. They assembled the book from the various places where the illustrations ended up, as they were never assembled into the original work for which they were intended.

José Gerónimo Triana was appointed botanist and was helped by other botanists like Hermann Karsten over a period of six years after which he left Codazzi, the commission, and the continent. Triana published a number of works, including *Flora de la Nueva Granada* with Karsten in 1855 and *Prodomus florae novogranatensis* with Planchón between 1862 and 1867.

11. Ardila, 12.

12. Santiago Pérez and Manuel Ancízar published their chronicles in newspapers; later, their works were collected in larger volumes. Other examples of the commission's work were published between 1850 and 1859 in the form of articles sent to official government publications as well as in the form of reports, letters, and maps by Codazzi to the governors of the provinces, and to the secretary of exterior relations. The bulk of these reports, letters, and maps, together with

tables and descriptions of the provinces, are collected in the four-volume work *Jeografía física i política de las provincias de la Nueva Granada por la Comisión Corográfica bajo la dirección de Agustín Codazzi (Physical and Political Geography of the Provinces of New Granada by the Chorography Commission under the Direction of Agustín Codazzi)*. It was published in 1856. Still other examples of the commission's works, mainly the maps and the results of Triana's botanical research, were published only after Codazzi's death in 1859.

13. Johannes Fabian reminds us that the fact that such travelogues manifest a preoccupation with the description of movements and relations in space does not preclude the contention that particular conceptions of time may be their underlying concern. Fabian. 7.

14. I borrow the central concepts of imagined communities and mapping from Angel Rama and Benedict Anderson.

15. Slavery was abolished in Colombia in 1851, and a second constitution was written in 1853 expanding provincial autonomy by giving the provinces power to elect their governors.

16. Pratt, "Scratches," 128.

17. The eye "commands" what falls within its gaze; the mountains "show themselves" or "present themselves"; the country "opens up" before the European newcomer, as does the unclothed indigenous bodyscape. Pratt, "Scratches," 124, 142 n.

18. The first volume of the original was published in 1814, in French, with the title *Relation historique aux régions équinoxiales du Noveau Continent*. My references are to Helen Maria Williams's translation, *Personal Narrative of Travels to the Equinoctial Regions of the New Continent during the Years 1799–1804* (London: Longman., 1822).

19. Such analogies would challenge the notions of leaders and intellectuals arguing for the inferiority of distinctly separate species, but they would also naturalize the hierarchies of the empirical mind. Gould, 30–39.

    In his earlier book (*Researches*, published in 1810), Humboldt argued that the American race was cut off from the rest of mankind. He described the American race as a race of wanderers, remote from civilization, in a long struggle against nature. *Researches*, 38–40. "Their countries, customs and institutions and arts differ from the Greeks and Romans as the primitive extinct race of animals differs from those of the species." *Researches*, 5.

20. González Echevarría, 395.

21. The culmination of his work was appropriately named *Kosmos*.

22. Humboldt points out that the Southern Cross is as much a literary reference for European writers like Dante and Bernardin Saint-Pierre as it is a cosmological reference point for the American guides he hired in his travels through Venezuela and Peru.

23. Humboldt confesses that the impulse for his eighteen years of planning was simply the desire to wander to the equinoctial regions, to see the Southern Cross, and to escape the sedentary life that he feared.

24. Humboldt, *Personal Narrative*, 2:292–93.

25. Ibid., 1:140.

26. Humboldt, *Researches*, 1–33.

27. The scene was sketched by Humboldt in 1801. The sketch was developed into a detailed landscape by Koch in Rome, and turned into a beautiful engraving by the house of Duttenhofer in Stuttgard. It was then published in an atlas that

accompanied the more luxurious editions of *Researches*, all of which suggests the aggressively commercial bent of the book.

28. Humboldt, *Researches,* 66–67.
29. Quoted by Gould, 38. See also Humboldt, *Researches,* 15.
30. Humboldt, *Researches,* 5, 15.
31. Ibid., 75.
32. The mutiny on the *Bounty* occurred on April 28, 1879. Humboldt's reference to Bligh appears in *Personal Narrative,* 2:244.
33. Arbelaez, 232.
34. Pratt, *Imperial,* 148.
35. Ibid., 149.
36. Ibid., 155.
37. Ibid., 187.
38. The first edition of Mollien's book was published in 1824. It was translated into English that same year. A year later, however, Mollien published a second edition, augmented and reorganized. My references are to this second edition. There is no English translation of this edition, though there is a translation into Spanish.
39. Mollien, 2:174.
40. Ibid., 2:211.
41. Ibid., 2:178. Jean Baptiste Boussingault, who traveled extensively through New Granada between 1822 and 1830, explicitly associated imbecility with the creole disease in a treatise on the causes of goiter, where he also argued that the disease posed a problem of the greatest political importance for the nation. Boussingault, 151.
42. While Mollien suggested that moving the African from Senegal to the Magdalena had further degenerated the black body, he also affirmed that its immunity to the insalubrious climate of the lowlands and the increase of its population threatened the supremacy of the creoles. The so-called "question of color" was, according to Mollien, one of the last problems to be resolved by the regional governments. Mollien, 2:288.
43. Ibid., 1:82. Mollien added this passage portraying Bolivar as a hero to the second edition of his book, probably to quell some of the criticism leveled against him by his South American readers, who did not like what he had to say about the emerging republics. The addition is evidence of the degree to which the lettered elites influenced and transformed what Pratt has called the European reinvention of America. It is also evidence of the mirrorlike nature of the relation between the European and the Euro-American reinventions: the European representation of America mirrors or is aligned with the Euro-American vision, while distorting it in the process.
44. Morel, 11.
45. Quoted by Pick, 46. The description clearly makes cretinism into an early medical form of degeneration in Europe.
46. Europe's rural population appeared to be distant in time from the modern metropolitan cities to these urbane travelers. This perceived distance led to a modernizing effort, or to an attempt at self-colonization: a process for turning "unruly" peasants into citizens. Pick, 40.
47. Mollien, 2:288.
48. I owe this description to E. A. Williams, quoted by Tapper, 63.
49. Tapper, 69–70.

50. Boussingault cites Humboldt as saying that American Indians, due to the purity of their race, are immune to goiter. Boussingault, 150. Mollien, echoing the scientific theories of his time states that neither "indians" nor "blacks" of pure race are prone to lymphatic illnesses. Mollien, 2:175.
51. Mollien, 2:194.
52. Mollien says that the Colombians answer his skepticism about their overtly optimistic predictions by showing him "the constant influx from England of money, immigrants and steam engines." Mollien, 2:287–88.
53. See Hugo Vezzetti's insightful discussion, and his ingenious description of Sarmiento's *Facundo, civilización y barbarie* as a grandiloquent project of civilization. Vezzetti, 95–97.
54. Following the failure of such projects, some of their proponents returned to the violent practices decried by the Chorography Commission, such as the outright elimination of "contaminating" bodies. Sarmiento would reach this conclusion in his last book, *Conflictos y harmonías de las razas en América Latina.*
55. Pratt, *Imperial,* 182.
56. See Benedict Anderson's insightful discussion of these fantasies and their legacy, 187–206.
57. Pick, 56.
58. Ancízar, 24, 486; Pombo, 143.
59. Ancízar, 24.
60. Caballero, 184, 209.
61. A more elaborate example of the use of allegory by Pérez to the same end is "La pirámide de la Itica-Pol." *Museo,* 3:65.
62. Codazzi, *Jeografía,* 292.
63. Pérez, in *Museo,* 2: 152.
64. Codazzi, *Jeografía,* 323.
65. Pick, 8.
66. For Pérez and Ancízar, the Tuqurreño and the Chibcha, respectively, were degenerate. Pérez, in *Museo,* 2:270; Ancízar, 27.
67. Codazzi, *Memorias,* 353–54.
68. Ibid., 359–60.
69. Codazzi, *Jeografía,* 409, 439.
70. Ibid., 344.
71. Ancízar, 48, 65, 137.
72. Alpha was the pseudonym used by Ancízar in *Peregrinación de Alpha.*
73. Pérez, in *Museo,* 4:175.
74. Ibid., 2:149.
75. Codazzi, *Jeografía,* 344.
76. Ancízar, 68.
77. Ibid., 82.
78. Codazzi, *Jeografía,* 333–34.
79. Pombo, 116.
80. Codazzi, *Jeografía,* 336.
81. Ibid., 437.
82. B. Anderson, 25.
83. Caballero, 147.
84. Pombo, 115.
85. Mollien vividly relates an incident on his way up the Magdalena river which makes him a hero in the eyes of his boatmen. The rope that secured Mollien's

canoe breaks in the middle of the rapids and the *bogas* or boatmen jump out of the boat, giving it up for lost. They also abandon Mollien, who does not know how to swim, inside the drifting canoe, leaving him to his own devices. "Deafened," writes Mollien "by the roaring of the waters and incensed by the cries of my fugitive boatmen, I leaped into the water which came up to my chin, and availing myself of an oar which I had seized at the moment of the accident, used it as a lever with which I lifted up the boat." Mollien, 1:63. See also illustrations of French travelers like André Edouard's for examples of the traveler as hero overcoming adversity.

86. David Guarín (1830–1890) was a Colombian short story writer and a poet whose "Un día de San Juan en tierra caliente" was published in *Museo*, 1:263.

87. Ancízar, 486.

2. Weaning the Virile Subject (pp. 48–68)

1. Other sets of oppositions are master/slave, self/other, law/nature, citizen/revolution, individual/nation, and solid/liquid.

   The series is invoked not only by the nineteenth-century texts that occupy us here. They are also conjured by present-day critical commentary about similar texts. In his book *The Lettered City*, Angel Rama represents the colonial cities described by Juan D. Sarmiento in his famous *Facundo, civilización y barbarie*, as virtual cities experiencing the pressures of the material reality surrounding them. The cities are compared to submerged bathyscaphes suffering the pressure of the water that surrounds them.

   In his essay on *Facundo*, Roberto González Echevarría similarly compares European travel accounts to the submarine of Captain Nemo, and sets that metaphorical capsule against the accidental and catachrestic language of literature. He marks the scientific model with rational attributes and the literary model with corporeal ones. While both models inform a text like *Facundo*, clearly the second is the stronger force acting on it, according to González Echevarría.

   In both critical essays there is a common series of gendered oppositions, the most significant one being that between male writing and female matter, or letter and liquid. It is from this founding conflict, or from that initial opposition, that both critics make their respective, very different judgments about the same nineteenth-century work.

2. Samper, 181.

3. Sarah is the wife of Abraham in the Book of Genesis. She was childless until she was ninety years old when she gave birth to Isaac. This fulfilled the promise God made to Abraham that he would be the founder of "a mighty nation."

   Doris Sommer's reading of *María* fleshes out the more than fortuitous similarity between the name of Sarah's offspring and the Colombian novelist Isaacs. In her compelling essay she makes pointed remarks about the contradictions that emerge from Isaacs's simultaneous meditation on the self and on race. Sommer, 172–203.

4. I owe this term, and much of my analysis here, to Kelly Oliver. She insightfully associates virility with culture, and therefore with a paradoxical sacrifice of the feminine and a rejection of the body. Oliver, *Family*, 120–33.

5. Quoted in Pick, 18.

6. Oliver, *Family*, 128.
7. Partial desuetude, atrophy, and degeneration, the loss of meaning and purpose—in short, death—must be numbered, Nietzsche argues, among the conditions of any true *progressus*, which later appears always in the form of the will and means to a greater power and is achieved at the expense of numerous lesser powers. Nietzsche, *Genealogy*, 210.
8. According to Stephen Jay Gould, degenerationists had the more popular argument because they did not discard Scripture lightly. On the other hand, Gould maintains that the polygenists had "the harder argument [because they] abandoned Scripture as allegorical and held that human races were separate biological species, the descendants of different Adams." Gould, 39.
9. In the first three chapters of Genesis, the law that assures the continuity of the species according to its primitive form is articulated in three different places, relating to both the animal and to the vegetable species: And God said, Let the earth bring forth the living creature after his kind, cattle, and creeping thing, and beast of the earth after his kind. (*Genesis* 2:24) (Morel, 2 n)
10. Stuart Gilman, 33.
11. Morel, 47. From this religious high ground, Morel argued against slavery, and defended what polygenists called inferior species against naturalists and anthropologists who were careless in their use of the concept of degeneration. Morel, 15–16. To argue that slavery was an immoral institution, Morel first conceded that there were clearly degenerate variations of a single original species, and that some of these were beyond regeneration. But he also argued that to admit as much was qualitatively different from saying that those degenerate races were a different species altogether. The original singularity of all of the races, even if some of them seemed inferior, made slavery an abhorrent institution.
12. Sander Gilman writes, "The theological model of the Fall as the wellspring of history and of Christ's sacrifice as mankind's redemption served as an explanation for human degeneration and regeneration." Gilman, *Difference*, 213.
13. Jeremiah 2:21.
14.

It may seem strange, at first, that I have not found it necessary to pose the fundamental question, to wit, whether the human species degenerates; the reason is simple enough: the question asked in such terms is unanswerable or maybe it is poorly framed. Indeed, insofar as the destiny of humanity is fixed by the wisdom of God, we cannot conceive of applying the term degeneration in its most rigorous meaning to the whole of the human species. According to our definition, degeneration is the infirm deviation from a primitive normal type; but progress, which is the objective of the life of humanity, is incompatible with such a situation. (Morel, 360–61)

15. He agreed with the French philosopher Condillac when he remarked "of all the created beings, the least likely to make mistakes, is that with the smallest amount of brains." Moreau, 487.
16. "If man degenerates physically due to mental exertion, he perfects himself morally." Moreau, 473.
17. "For, if it is true that through meditation and reflection, through a great tension in the wheels of the mind, a man endowed with great moral faculties has a tendency to deteriorate physically, and to intensify, as a result, an innate and morbid predisposition, then similarly it is true that he improves or perfects himself in

that part of his self that is most noble, that part through which he is really a man, that is to say a soul wearing a body, or, following a famous definition: an intelligence ruling over the organs." Moreau, 473.

18. Gilman, *Difference*, 207.
19. Ibid., 213.
20. Ibid., 210.
21. Oliver, *Family*, 34–66.
22. Freud, *Sexuality*, 212–13.
23. Freud, *Character*, 69.
24. Ibid., 74–75.
25. Ibid., 78–79.
26. See Oliver's convincing argument on this point, which is based on Hegel's purposeful use of the figure of Antigone. Oliver, *Family*, 39.
27. *Museo*, 8–9.
28. Samper, 60.
29. Ibid., 26.
30. Ibid., 114–15.
31. Ibid., 49, 187.
32. Examples of these events are the indistinct mass (or the individual-lacking collectivity), the feudal and land-owning systems, and the monarchy based on a corrupt aristocracy.
33. See Samper's fascinating discussion of the *resguardos*, the Spanish American version of the Indian reservation. Samper, 64–65.
34. Ibid., 64.
35. Sommer, 172–203.
36. The thematic struggle between duplicity and integrity, chance and steadfastness, are explored in the biblical story of Esther, after whom María was originally named.

    María's duplicitous simulation has been remarked by critics like Gustavo Mejía, who points out the subversive effect of Efraín's conversations with the various women in the novel on paternal authority and hierarchy. Isaacs, xiv–xv. This critic, however, sees these events in the novel as signs of Isaacs's decadence, and of the degeneration of the social class to which he belongs. Far from naturalizing the event that is degeneration or decadence, we are here more concerned with its deployment and use in the novel itself. It is nonetheless interesting that Isaacs's discourse on degeneration and decadence has been perpetuated by the criticism about his novel, to the point of becoming an ideological weapon wielded against him.
37. Isaacs, 192.
38. Ibid., 20.
39. From this perspective, it is equally significant that in an earlier scene Efraín has to battle an enraged river to reach a doctor, right after María's first epileptic attack.
40. Samper, 77–79.
41. Ibid., 45, 48.
42. Ibid., 49.
43. Ibid., 218, 220.
44. Ibid., 198, 218.
45. Ibid., 218.
46. Ibid., 217.

47. Isaacs, 109.

48. In *Desencuentros de la modernidad,* Julio Ramos describes the difference between the travel chronicles written by so-called patrician writers such as Juan D. Sarmiento, and those by *modernistas* like José Martí. According to Ramos, the *modernista* travel account has a different relationship to catastrophe than its Romantic counterpart. For writers like Sarmiento this difference is based on his optimism about the future of Spanish America. For Sarmiento, catastrophe is a fortuitous event that provides a clearing space in which the notions of modernity and progress can take physical shape. For writers like Martí, on the other hand, catastrophe is a metaphor for modernity itself, perhaps best summarized as the collapse of the values held dear by the earlier patricians, and still held dear by the emerging classes of professionals.

    Ramos's analysis provides one possible and compelling interpretation of the function of catastrophe and crisis in these works. There is no doubt that Sarmiento projects onto Argentina a figure of himself, confidently going toward an imminent future, from a present full of problems and possibilities. In *Facundo,* Sarmiento conjures the murdered Facundo Quiroga, to tell his story as a parable for the sins of the past that must not be repeated. In the telling, however, the narrator also suggests an attraction and a respect for that past that, according to the logic of the same work, must spell disaster not only for its protagonist, but also for the narrator himself. From that perspective the work is both a museum piece preserved to be contemplated as an awe-inspiring reminder, and a sign of the future that threatens Argentina.

    A similar set of lessons is found in Isaacs's novel. His work also is a similar nostalgic exercise in which the dead are conjured from the present. The past is there conjured as an original moment of catastrophe that makes room for a tabula rasa on which the future can be written. The past is a familiar moment of origin to which the narrator, presumably now living in London, cannot return. Thus Isaacs devotes much space in that work to recreating the past down to its smallest detail. By the end the narrator has in effect written a relic to take with him to Europe, a relic that reminds him, and maybe relieves him, of the responsibility of leaving and forgetting the point of origin. But the novel can also be read as a guilty response to the accusation leveled at the narrator by María: that Efraín could have chosen to stay with her in Colombia, instead of leaving her and thereby causing her untimely death. *María* can then be read as the attempt of an unforgiven conscience to show contrition for an act that is unforgivable.

    In both these works, then, time is recovered. Disappeared figures are shaped into portable objects, like books, to serve the reader and the writer as memento mori. These monuments to the past are both liberating and condemning exercises. They are the temporal remains of the paradox we are diagnosing here.

49. Efraín travels back and forth from Europe with boxes filled with books, and is often shown reading. The aura surrounding books, and the metaphorical network cast by Samper and Isaacs, reaches the figure of Isaacs himself, and is perpetuated by it. Isaacs's biographies rely on the aura of this network to project him to the level of myth. Arciniegas's biography offers a number of head shots of Isaacs, as well as a photograph taken of him when he was twenty-one years old, holding both a patrician pose and a voluminous book. The cover of Velasco Madriñan's biography shows Issacs's head framed by a book. The cover is, in turn, a slightly modified version of the novelist's tombstone in the city of Medellín.

50. Quoted in Arciniegas, 37.
51. See Ignacio Gutiérrez Vergara's "Cachaco," in *Museo*, 1:195–99; David Guarín's "Un día de San Juan en tierra caliente," in *Museo*, 1:263–379; José M. Marroquín's "La carrera de mi sobrino," in *Museo*, 2:159–70.
52. Gutiérrez Vergara, in *Museo*, 1:196.
53. Isaacs, 54.
54. See Sylvia Molloy's suggestive meditation on the connection between modernity and a brutal economy of loss in Isaacs's novel. Molloy, *Paraíso*, 36–55.
55. Oliver, *Womanizing*, 115–19.
56. Ibid., 115–16.

3. Anemia, Witches, and Vampires (pp. 69–88)

1. Unlike the majority of Latin America, Puerto Rico was not an independent republic by the end of the nineteenth century, but remained a Spanish colony. I borrow the term *letrado* from Angel Rama. He uses it to describe not only a class of cultured intellectuals, but also a particular type of colonized consciousness that accepts the arbitrariness of the connection, and therefore the implied rupture, between signs and referents.
2. Recent critical thinking on the Puerto Rican nation has emphasized the interdependence between the discourses of the Self and the construction of the Other. These cultural critics do not agree on the kind of mental representation that was constructed in order to empower the emerging governing class. José Luis González (195) claims that this intellectual class constructed the dystopia of an infirm social organism in need of regeneration; Angel G. Quintero Rivera (55–58) posits the utopia of an inherently harmonic and healthy social organism in need of some guidance. These apparent differences, however, can be reconciled.

    The *letrado*'s utopia (described by Quintero Rivera) gives a manageable place to the "black" body of the newly freed slave in the lower rungs of the social hierarchy, even as it helps to establish a figurative common ground from which the nation can be represented as diseased (González's dystopia), but with a curable illness. Thus, the related figures of the anemic peasant woman and of illness as a metaphor for the "black" body emerge from that figurative common ground as versions of an Other, conjured to authorize the figure of a national Self.

    While the reconciliation of these thought-provoking analyses goes some distance in the attempt to explain the event of constructing a nation by the *letrados*, it does not go far enough, because it does not successfully interpret the disfiguring force within the *letrado*'s discourse of Self. In this essay, I attempt to do just that by going beyond a description of the interrelation between the utopic figure of a Puerto Rican harmonious Self and the dystopic figure of a Puerto Rican infirm Other. Instead, I have set these figures against the competing figures for Self and Other that were constructed by the metropolitan forces, thus returning its complexity to the *letrado*'s self-figuration as a part of a nation in perpetual crisis.
3. In this chapter, skin color is put in quotation marks because color is here understood to be a discursive marker of racial difference, and not a physical trait, not unlike the teeth of the parasite "seen" by the local *letrados*, described in the introduction to this book and revisited at the end of this chapter. The quotation

marks are meant to call attention to and to call into question this discrete, but generalized, way of ordering and governing bodies. I owe my understanding of color and race to Melbourne Tapper, who convincingly argues that "race and ethnicity are always discoursive practices." My analysis of anemia also owes much to Tapper's claim that diseases like sickle-cell anemia are discoursive practices of anthropology and medical science, and are used for the purposes of distinguishing between two races. Tapper, "Interrogating Bodies," 178.

4. They both published in liberal periodicals (*El asimilista, La revista puertorriqueña*), and were part of the liberal intellectual group that not only gathered at the library of José González Font, but also published numerous works in his printing press. See Fernández Méndez's introduction to Brau, *Disquisiciones sociológicas* 79–80; Quintero Rivera, 198 n. Four works are most significant here. Two are scientific memoirs about the Puerto Rican peasant, which were awarded prizes by the Ateneo Puertorriqueño: Francisco del Valle Atiles, *El campesino puertorriqueño* (1887), and Salvador Brau, "Las clases jornaleras" originally published in 1882, and later included in *Disquisiciones sociológicas*. The other two, Atiles's "La comadre que medra" (1883) and Brau's ¿*Pecadora*? (1887), are literary works. Both are considered to be predecessors of Puerto Rico's most important naturalist work, *La charca*, published in 1896 by the physician-writer Manuel Zeno Gandía.

5. I borrow the term "laboratory medicine" from Warwick Anderson who uses it to mean the type of medicine that was practiced principally in the laboratory, as opposed to a medical practice that was centered around the consultory. Anderson's Foucauldian emphasis on "laboratory medicine," rather than on changes in the object of scientific analysis (as in the term "tropical medicine"), appropriately foregrounds the importance of medical practice.

6. Picó, *Historia general*, 193–96.

7. Yellow fever killed governor-generals Vega Inclán and José Gamir, in 1884 and 1898, respectively.

8. See Fernández Méndez's introduction to Brau, *Disquisiciones sociológicas*, 81–103.

9. Quoted in Brau, "La campesina," *Disquisiciones*, 219–20.

10. Ferrer, 35. Gabriel Ferrer (1847–1900) was an influential liberal reformist physician-writer, whose ideas clearly reflected the scientific commonplaces of the times and whose work on the Puerto Rican woman influenced the writings of both Atiles and Brau.

11. Stuart Gilman, 39.

12. Picó, *Al filo*, 49. The works continuously cited to construct the figure of the Puerto Rican peasant as a vagrant were mainly the *Historia de Puerto Rico* by Fray Iñigo Abad, and the *Memoir* presented by Alejandro O'Reylly in 1765 to the Spanish government.

13. *Boletín oficial del Ministerio de Ultramar* 1874, cited in Brau, "Las clases jornaleras," *Disquisiciones*, 168–71.

14. Brau, "Las clases jornaleras," *Disquisiciones*, 170.

15. Picó, *Al filo*, 50–51.

16. This argument was based on the North American scientific writings on degeneracy after the Civil War. See Stuart Gilman, 30–31.

17. Atiles, *El campesino*, 73–75.

18. Brau, "Las clases jornaleras," *Disquisiciones*, 129.

19. I borrow this title from Susan Sontag's suggestive work.

20. Brau, "Las clases jornaleras," *Disquisiciones,* 127, 160.
21. Brau, *La vuelta,* 225; Brau, "Las clases jornaleras," *Disquisiciones,* 159.
22. Brau, "Las clases jornaleras," *Disquisiciones,* 145.
23. Predictably, this invisibility is explained in the novel as the result of the irresponsibility of the local authorities, who have abandoned all attempts at modernizing the communications network joining the small communities of the island.
24. See Quintero Rivera's analysis of Brau's study of popular music. Quintero Rivera, 220–29.
25. Brau, *La vuelta,* 207.
26. Brau, *La vuelta,* 205.
27. Atiles, *La salud,* 8.
28. Atiles, *El campesino,* 46–47.
29. Ibid., 58.
30. Ibid., 42–43.
31. See Atiles, "Eugénica," 1–4. See also by Atiles "Limitación," 1–7, and "Eugenesis," 9–21. In his most telling statements on the racial question, Atiles simultaneously "concedes" that even the inferior "black race" has something to offer the future of the Puerto Rican nation, and argues that "The peoples made up of inferior races, inept, decadent . . . are incompatible with the physical and mental activity that the law of progress imposes, and therefore are incompatible with progress itself." See Atiles, "Puerto Rico ante la eugénica," 65, 73–74.
32. Chlorosis gave medical form to a concern with the suppression or irregularity of the menses due to overrefinement, and was displayed by a loss of the natural color (thus its Greek etymology which means literally "a making green").
33. Figlio, 167–97.
34. Atiles, *La salud,* 105–9; 121–23.
35. Atiles understood not only that the white fetus was an unborn child, but also that it was the representation of the origins of the Puerto Rican nation. This made its abortion a doubly criminal practice, and turned delinquent the midwife's "parasitic" behavior.
36. The dangerous appropriation of a technical and incomprehensible medical language by the midwife is ridiculed in "La médica," a later story by Atiles about the same figure.
37. Atiles, *La salud,* 121.
38. Such at least was Atiles's intent when he described it as an unnecessarily "harsh" discourse, on the first page of the first volume of his 1883 publication *La salud,* significantly subtitled, "Hygienic Weekly within Everyone's Reach."
39. Manuel Alonso was one of the members of this group. He was also one of the leaders of the generation of *letrados* who introduced the figure of the infirm peasant in his collection of short works entitled *El Jíbaro.* A succinct description of this emerging group of doctors and their difference from popular and local medical practice is found in Atiles's *Biografía de Franciso J. Hernández.*
40. In both *¿Pecadora?,* and "The Midwife Who Prospers," the narrator mocks a midwife's description of disease as "air with blood." See Brau, *La vuelta,* 187; and Atiles, *La salud,* 106.
41. See Douglas, 85.
42. For a detailed description of the meanings of "aire" in the anthropological literature see Kearney, 46–58; and Adams and Rubel.
43. Kearney, 49.
44. Ashford, *A Soldier in Science,* 5. See Coll y Toste's *Tratamiento de la fiebre ama-*

rilla as an example of the same laboratory medicine predating the invasion by the United States.

45. Ancylostomiasis is a disease caused by the loss of blood from the small intestine; it causes anemia, constipation, and diarrhea.
46. Quevedo Baez.
47. Ashford, "De la liga," 123. Also see Stahl, 161.
48. One important consequence of this qualitative turn in the disciplining strategies would be the creation of a rift within the *letrado* establishment between those who followed the political implications of a new treatment based on strategic intervention (these doctors started a campaign for building sites of micromanagement and self-control called anemia camps throughout the countryside), and those who remained suspicious of the practice and chose instead to continue their efforts to build on a less diffuse form of control and discipline. Space constraints, however, make it impossible to develop the implications of this division; I will have to postpone this discussion.
49. See Stepan and Gilman.
50. The crisis represented by the anemic state of the Puerto Rican peasant woman is but one version of the paradoxical ordering of a world by constructing it as heterogeneous. Indeed, the perception of a crisis is the fiction upon which authority is founded. The construction of a crisis is empowering; it creates the need for a mediator, or moderator, that can settle in the space opened by the rupture. But a crisis is also disempowering; it overdetermines the figure of a naturalized citizen. For a discussion of the concept of citizenship along these lines, please see Warwick Anderson; Quintero Rivera; and Julio Ramos, "A Citizen Body."

4. Crossing the Boundaries of Madness (pp. 90–102)

1. See Canguilhem, *Ideology and Rationality*, 27–40.
2. Ingenieros, *La locura*, 9.
3. Ramos Mejía, *Las neurosis*, xii.
4. Foucault, *Birth*, 3–21.
5. Sarmiento, 100.
6. Stigmata are bodily marks or pains resembling the wounds of the crucified Christ and sometimes accompanying religious ecstasy.
7. Juan Manuel de Rosas was an Argentinian politician who was described as a dictator by his liberal counterparts. He was the head of the Federalist party, and became the governor of the province of Buenos Aires from 1829–1832. He remained in power, in effect, until 1852.
8. Ramos Mejía, *Las neurosis*, 104.
9. López Piñero, 113.
10. In Genesis, Cain is doubly marked by God, first in punishment for the murder of Abel, and second in pity for Cain's cry for mercy. It is significant here that God's mark makes Cain both cursed and divine to common men.
11. For further comment on the Western representation of the womb as a passive container instead of an active agent, consult chapter 1 of Oliver, *Family Values*.
12. Ramos Mejía, *La locura*, 96–97.
13. And yet the thorn is never quite encysted, and thus it is difficult to locate, which suggests the budding paradoxical notion of invisible stigmata, which will lead Ingenieros to abandon the effort to locate them altogether.

14. The italics are in the original. Ramos Mejía, "Medicina legal," 430.
15. Ingenieros was concerned with keeping two groups of insane criminals apart be-cause they required different strategies: treatment and eventual freedom for the criminal with acquired insanity versus perpetual sequestration and death for the criminal with genetic insanity. The simulator threatened to confuse these cate-gories, thus making the criminal not only a danger to society, but also turning him into a problem for criminologists, making proper treatment almost impos-sible.
16. For an exhaustive discussion of the construction of the genre of the scientific paper, see Markus.
17. Ingenieros, *La simulación*, 11–12.
18. Ramos Mejía, *La locura*, xxi.
19. Ramos Mejía, *Las neurosis*, 64.
20. At one point, Ingenieros called the reader's attention to the ideologically charged rhetorical strategy that gave form to Ramos Mejía's psychiatric history of Juan Manuel de Rosas in *Las neurosis*, which links that work to Sarmiento's famous, politically biased *Facundo*. After pointing to Ramos Mejía's careless use of Eduardo Gutierrez's "terrorist pamphlets," Ingenieros goes so far as to quote Sarmiento's own introduction to the first edition of *Las neurosis*, in which Sar-miento cautions the young Ramos Mejía against innocently trusting all accusa-tions made against Rosas. See Ramos Mejía, *Las neurosis*, 18–19.
21. In his 1895 introduction to Ramos Mejía's *La locura*, Paul Groussac questions the existence of these lesions. Both Groussac and Ingenieros followed the physiopathological model, first delineated by Francois-Joseph Victor Broussais (1772–1838) in his popular *Examination of Medical Doctrines* (1816), which suggested that the abnormality of the diseased brain of the criminal was specific and could be scientifically measured, but was functional, not morphological, in nature.
22. In an article about the psychology of writers published in 1908, Ingenieros com-pared the human brain to a daguerreotype. His emphasis on the brain as a ma-chine underscored the radical materialism of the new criminological school: its continuing willingness to think of the human mind primarily as matter. But his stress on the brain's moving and complementary parts, on its intrinsic adaptabil-ity to outside influence, illustrated by the image of light hitting a sensitive photo-graphic plate, was the result of his school's interest in function versus form, and of its shift of emphasis from what Ingenieros described as a morphological etiol-ogy of madness to a sociological one. Ingenieros, "Variedades," 583.
23. Ingenieros's shift away from a verbally centered scientific discourse was also at the center of his criticism of organicism in sociology. Ingenieros wrote:

    Biological Sociology lets us explain genetically the evolution of human societies . . . The natural development of human societies can be understood if we replace this classical Spencerian "Organicism" with a biological interpretation of social evolution. Society is nothing more than "colonies organized by the division of so-cial functions". It is not a "superorganism" . . . Biological sociology takes back the problem to its most general and biological form. Instead, organicist sociologists limit themselves to an explanation through analogy. (Quoted in Soler, 199)

24. As Hugo Vezzetti has argued, Ingenieros became more interested in the techni-cal and legal function of managing crime and insanity (distinguishing between

different types of insane criminals in a court of justice, and treating them in appropriate institutions) than in identifying and sequestering the deranged, which was the generic function of the earlier moralizing school of legal medicine. Vezzetti, 127–84.

25. Ingenieros, "Valor," 7.
26. The first signs of the formal organization of bacteriology as a science came in 1876 with the discovery by Robert Koch that anthrax, an illness affecting both cattle and humans, was caused by bacteria. At that time the study of bacteria took two directions: the German school was headed by Koch and the French school by Pasteur. The former is of greater interest here because it emphasized the study and development of technical methods to examine and cultivate bacteria, and because its results were intended for prophylactic purposes. Ingenieros celebrated and implemented these techniques, which consisted of a strategy simultaneously nurturing and vigilant, and which aimed at stimulating instruments of self-control within the insane.
27. Ingenieros's work was not consistent on this point. He also distinguished between two types of criminals, and two kinds of therapy adequate to each type of criminal. For Ingenieros the violent, and often deadly, treatment diagnosed for the hereditary criminal was still appropriate, but only to a small segment of the insane population. But the bulk of the social problem lay, for Ingenieros, inside the mind of the criminal whose insanity was acquired, and who could be reformed using a therapeutic version of the techniques of bacteriology.
28. The parasitic theory of illness was the outcome of a challenge to the theory of spontaneous generation, which led to the discovery of the filarial worm in the late 1870s, and of the true biological host in 1900.
29. Soto-Hall, 299–300.
30. Riaño Jauma, 106–7.
31. Ingenieros, *Dos páginas,* 75–76.
32. Bagú, 86.
33. Quoted in Bagú, 97–98.

5. The Crisis of Memory (pp. 104–123)

1. See also Nietzsche, *Genealogy,* 57–96.
2. Taine, 108.
3. The magic lantern, wheel of life, or zoetrope was a popular toy during the 1880s. It induced the illusion of movement from pictures drawn or painted on a revolving mirror, which were projected by means of an oil lamp onto a rotating drum. It was a predecessor of the motion picture camera.

   In Proust's novel, the magic lantern is a gift intended as a distraction during wretched, melancholy and anxious evenings. Instead, the zoetrope's substitution of fantastic scenes for the opaqueness of the walls and objects of the familiar room is first a fragmenting and then a dizzying experience both frightening and fascinating the narrator. Proust, 9.
4. Proust, 6.
5. Zeno de Matos, 42.
6. Zeno Gandía, *Higiene de la infancia,* 10–11.
7. Ibid., 15.
8. For an insightful analysis of this collapse, consult Rose, "Medicine," 48–72.

9. Zeno Gandía, *Higiene de la infancia*, 6.
10. Zeno Gandía's image of the female mind as a magic lantern also appeared in the doctoral work on anemia of yet another Puerto Rican writer and physician. José de Jesús Domínguez, a practicing surgeon trained in Paris and a modernist poet, wrote in 1871 that:

> Anemia invariably makes women hysterical to some degree, one could even suggest that hysteria is nothing but a sign of anemia . . . Women wounded by this malady become unbearable to those around them. Its signs are sadness and happiness without a cause, weeping alternating with bursts of laughter, dark thoughts at times, absurdly colorful ideas at other times; in short a hysterical woman is a magic lantern. (Domínguez, 51)

11. Zeno Gandía, *La charca*, 2.
12. Celluloid film was manufactured successfully in 1888 by George Eastman.
13. Ibid., 161–62.
14. Ibid., 136.
15. Nietzsche, *Twilight*, 61–62.
16. Zeno Gandía, *La charca*, 15.
17. Ibid., 18.
18. Ibid., 14.
19. Ibid., 158.
20. Ibid., 18.
21. Silva, *Obra completa*, 254–56.
22. The sinecure resulted from Silva's political connections, and was a measure of the corrupt and liberal nature of the administration that just as easily had flexed its political muscle the year before, declaring a state of siege in the Colombian capital. The year of Silva's appointment, that same administration suffered perhaps its most severe economic and political setback. A clandestine emission of currency by its national bank forced the national bank's closure.
23. Silva, *Obra completa*, 271.
24. According to Nordau, consciousness, or the Ego, emerges at the center of all the nerve ducts, where the nerve paths of the body meet. The ducts are the physical traces left by the repeated passage of the disturbance, which follows the map back to the brain. With time, these ducts become wider and more marked, as the map becomes literally imprinted on the tissue. This process also inscribes the brain of the young consciousness. The brain is itself an indentation, a depth, a concavity, a room, created by the habitual repetition of a memorized return to itself. Nordau, 45–54.
25. Ibid., 52, 54.
26. Ibid., 477.
27. Memory, then, suspends time and fragments space into successive negative and positive impressions. But memory also produces time flow by creating the difference between a past event recorded in a negative image, and a present event that exposes the earlier image and creates a positive one.
28. This, in turn, produced the first association, in Fernández's mind, between the positive image of the painting and Helena. Viewing Helena further produced a negative imprint associated with the positive image of the painting. Viewing the painting a second time did not stimulate the exposure of its own negative; instead it stimulated the exposure of the negative of Helena, and its earlier association

with the memory image of the painting. This composite memory image then became the mistaken confirmation of an identity between the painting and Helena. This identity, then, led Fernández to think that Helena was the original of the painting, when in fact, she was but a negative copy stimulated by the painting into a positive image.

29. See Rose, *Inventing*, 112; Sander Gilman, *Disease*, 18–49.
30. Saint Ignatius of Loyola was the founder of the religious order of the Jesuits. He was also the author of the *Spiritual Exercises*, a famous set of mystical instructions to help the layman achieve spiritual enlightenment. The *Exercises* are still a preferred text used by the Jesuits during retreats organized by them for their communities.
31. Loyola, 23.
32. Silva, *Obra completa*, 128.
33. Her day begins with a reading of Balzac and ends with verses from the Psalms. She paints and plays the piano. She thinks of sculpting and traveling. Silva, *Obra completa*, 121–24.
34. Ibid., 121.
35. Ibid., 123.
36. The same process can be found in symbolist and decadent works written before Zeno Gandía's manual, such as "The Voyage" (1857) or Huysman's *Against Nature* (1884), in that it educates and disciplines a masculine mind. The poetic subject in *Flowers of Evil* compares the reader to a boy and invites him on a symbolist grand tour lit by "the blaze of the lamps." Des Esseintes's imaginary journey leaves the traveler "feeling all the physical weariness and moral fatigue of *a man* who has come home after a long and perilous journey."
37. Silva, *Obra completa*, 123, 127.
38. Kristeva, 85–91.
39. Ibid., 86.
40. Ibid., 91.
41. Freud, *Early Psychoanalytic Writings*, 235.
42. Ibid., 229.
43. Rose, *Inventing*, 37.
44. Ibid.
45. Silva, *Obra completa*, 188.
46. Ibid., 243.
47. Molloy, *At Face Value*, 20.
48. Ibid., 3–4.
49. *La charca* was written by Manuel Zeno Gandía (a Puerto Rican doctor and politician) during a period of persecution and repression by the appointed military governors of the former Spanish colony. The period would culminate three years later (in 1897) in a short-lived autonomous government headed by the members of the liberal pro-autonomy party persecuted under colonial rule. After the colony was lost to the United States during the Spanish-American War, the autonomous government was replaced by military rule. But it would serve as one of the models for the liberal commonwealth later established in the territory.

De sobremesa was written by José Asunción Silva, a businessman and politician, during a period of similar persecution and repression under the authoritarian republic of Rafael Nuñez. The period, known as a conservative attempt at national regeneration, was marked by liberal rebellions. It culminated in 1899 in the War of a Thousand Days, which raged for three years and ended in a victory by the conservative government, a victory which nevertheless reformed the conservative republic over the next thirty years.

50. By mnemotechniques I mean what Rose (following Nietzsche) calls devices "by which one 'burns' the past into oneself and makes it available as a warning, a comfort, a bargaining device, a weapon, or a wound." Rose, *Inventing,* 179–80.

Conclusion (pp. 125–127)

1. Tapper, 59.
2. Rose, *Inventing,* 12.
3. Romero, 118–19.
4. Foucault, "Subject," 213–15.
5. "Clinton Proposes IMF Act Earlier to Prevent Crises," David E. Sanger, *New York Times,* October 3, 1998, A1
6. "Excerpts from Minority Counsel Presentation to House Judiciary Committee," *New York Times,* October 6, 1998, A23.

Bibliography

Acevedo, Eduardo Latorre. *Fabulous Colombia's Geography: The New Grenade* [sic] *as Seen by Two French Travellers of the XIX Century: Charles Saffray, Eduard André.* Bogotá: Litografía Arco, 1980.

Adams, Richard N., and Arthur J. Rubel. "Sickness and Social Relations." In *Handbook of Middle American Indians,* ed. Robert Wauchope, 6: 333–56. Austin: University of Texas Press, 1964.

Alonso, Carlos, *The Spanish American Regional Novel.* Oxford: Cambridge University Press, 1990.

Ancízar, Manuel. *Peregrinación de Alpha por las provincias del norte de Nueva Granada 1850–51.* Bogotá: La Empresa Nacional de Publicaciones, 1956.

Anderson, Benedict. *Imagined Communities.* London: Verso, 1993.

Anderson, Warwick. "Where Every Prospect Pleases and Only Man Is Vile: Laboratory Medicine as Colonial Discourse." *Critical Inquiry* 18 (1992): 506–29.

Arbelaez, Enrique Pérez. *Alejandro Humboldt en Colombia.* Bogotá: Editorial Iqueima, 1959.

Arciniegas, Germán. *Genio y figura de Jorge Isaacs.* Buenos Aires: Editorial Universitaria, 1967.

Ardila, Jaime, and Camilo Lleras. *Batalla contra el olvido.* Bogotá: Ardila y Lleras, 1985.

Ashford, Bailey K. "De la liga contra la urcinariasis en Puerto Rico." *Boletín de la Asociación Médica de Puerto Rico* 3, no. 32 (1905): 119–25.

———. *A Soldier in Science.* New York: William Morrow, 1934.

Atiles, Francisco del Valle. *Biografía de Francisco J. Hernández y Martínez, doctor en medicina y cirugía.* Puerto Rico: Imprenta de José González Font, 1885.

———. *El campesino puertorriqueño sus condiciones físicas, intelectuales y morales, causas que las determinan y medios para mejorarlas.* San Juan: Tipografía de José González Font, 1887.

———. "Eugenesis la base más firme de nuestro progreso." *Conferencias dominicales dadas en la biblioteca insular,* 9–21. San Juan: Bureau of Supplies, Printing and Transportation, 1914.

———. "Eugénica." *Boletín de la Asociación Médica de Puerto Rico* 10, no. 95 (1914): 1–4.

———. "Limitación de la prole." *Boletín de la Asociación Médica de Puerto Rico* 13, no. 114 (1917): 1–7.

———. "La médica." *Ilustración puertorriqueña* 1, no. 2 (1892).

———. "Puerto Rico ante la eugnica." *Conferencias dominicales dadas en la biblioteco insular.* 56–84. San Juan: Bureau of Supplies, Printing, and Transportation, 1914.

———. *La salud.* Puerto Rico: Imprenta las Bellas Letras, 1883.

Bagú, Sergio. *Vida ejemplar de José Ingenieros.* Buenos Aires: Librería el Ateneo, 1953.

Baudelaire, Charles. *The Flowers of Evil.* Ed. Marthiel and Jackson Mathews. New York: New Directions, 1989.

Boussingault, Jean Baptiste, and François Desire Roulin. *Viajes científicos a los andes ecuatoriales.* Trans. J. Acosta. Paris: Lasserre, 1849.

Brau, Salvador. *Disquisiciones sociológicas.* Río Piedras: Ediciones del Instituto de Literatura, 1956.

———. *La vuelta al hogar y ¿Pecadora?* Río Piedras: Editorial EDIL, 1975.

Caballero, Beatríz. *Las siete vidas de Agustín Codazzi.* Bogotá: Carlos Valencia Editores, 1994.

Canguilhem, Georges. *Ideology and Rationality in the History of the Life Sciences.* Trans. Arthur Goldhammer. Cambridge: MIT Press, 1988.

———. *The Normal and the Pathological.* Trans. Carolyn R. Fawcett in collaboration with Robert S. Cohen. New York: Zone Books, 1989.

Codazzi, Agustín. *Memorias de Agustín Codazzi.* Ed. Mario Longhena. Trans. Andres Soriano Lleras and Fr. Alberto Lee López. Bogotá: Talleres Gráficos del Banco de la República, 1973.

———. *Jeografía física i política de las provincias de la Nueva Granada por la Comisión Corográfica bajo la dirección de Agustín Codazzi.* 4 vols. Bogotá: Publicaciones del Banco de la República, 1959.

Coll y Toste, Cayetano. *Tratamiento de la fiebre amarilla.* Puerto Rico: Tipografía al vapor de "La Correspondencia," 1895.

Cook, Noble David. *Born to Die: Disease and New World Conquest, 1492–1650.* Cambridge: Cambridge University Press, 1988.

Delaporte, François. *Disease and Civilization: The Cholera in Paris, 1832.* Cambridge: MIT Press, 1986.

Doerner, Klaus. *Madmen and the Bourgeoisie: A Social History of Insanity and Psychiatry.* Trans. Joachim Neugroschel and Jean Steinberg. Oxford: Basil Blackwell, 1981.

Domínguez, José de Jesús. *Anémie idiopathique. Thèse pour le doctorat en médecine.* Paris: A. Parent, 1871.

Donato, Eugenio. "The Ruins of Memory: Archaeological Fragments and Textual Artifacts." *MLN* 93 (1978):575–96.

Douglas, Mary. "Witchcraft and Leprosy, Two Strategies for Rejection." *Working Papers in Cultural Studies, 70–89.* Cultural Studies Project. Cambridge: Massachusetts Institute of Technology, 1990.

Fabian, Johannes. *Time and the Other: How Anthropology Makes Its Object.* New York: Columbia University Press, 1983.

Fanon, Frantz. *Black Skin, White Masks.* Trans. Charles Lam Markmann. New York: Grove Wiedenfeld, 1967.

Ferrer, Gabriel. *La mujer en Puerto Rico. Sus necesidades presentes y los medios mas fáciles y adecuados para mejorar su porvenir.* Puerto Rico: Imprenta de "El Agente," 1881.

Figlio, Karl. "Chlorosis and Chronic Disease in Nineteenth-Century Britain: The Social Constitution of Somatic Illness in a Capitalist Society." *Social History* 3 (1978): 167–97.

Foucault, Michel. *The Birth of the Clinic: An Archeology of Medical Perception.* Trans. Tavistock Publications. New York: Vintage Books, 1973.

——. "The Order of Discourse." In *Untying the Text: A Post-Structuralist Reader,* ed. Robert Young. Boston: Routledge, 1981.

——. "The Subject and Power." In *Michel Foucault: Beyond Structuralism and Hermeneutics,* eds. Hubert L. Dreyfus and Paul Rabinow, 208–16. Chicago: University of Chicago Press, 1982.

——. "What Is an Author." In *Textual Strategies: Perspectives in Post-Structural Criticism,* ed. Josué Harari. Ithaca: Cornell University Press, 1979.

Freud, Sigmund. *Character and Culture.* Ed. Philip Rieff. New York: Collier Books, 1963.

——. *Early Psychoanalytic Writings.* Ed. Philip Rieff. New York: Collier Books, 1963.

——. *Sexuality and the Psychology of Love.* Ed. Philip Rieff. New York: Collier Books, 1963.

Gilman, Sander. *Difference and Pathology.* Ithaca: Cornell University Press, 1985.

——. *Disease and Representation: Images of Illness from Madness to AIDS.* Ithaca and London: Cornell University Press, 1988.

Gilman, Stuart. "Degeneracy and Race in the Nineteenth Century: The Impact of Clinical Medicine." *Journal of Ethics Studies* 10, no. 4 (1983): 27–50.

González Echevarría, Roberto. "Redescubrimiento del mundo perdido: el *Facundo* de Sarmiento." *Revista iberoamericana* 43 (1988): 385–406.

González, Anibal. "Turbulencias en *La Charca:* de Lucrecio a Manuel Zeno Gandía." *MLN* 98, no. 2 (1983):208–225.

González, José Luis. "Literatura e identidad nacional en Puerto Rico." In *Puerto Rico: identidad nacional y clases sociales,* ed. Angel Quintero Rivera. 45–79. Río Piedras: Ediciones Huracán, 1979.

Gould, Stephen Jay. *The Mismeasure of Man.* New York: W. W. Norton, 1993.

Habermas, Jürgen. *Toward a Rational Society.* Trans. Jeremy J. Shapiro. Boston: Beacon Press, 1970.

Humboldt, Alexander and A. Bondpland. *Personal Narrative of Travels to the Equinoctial Regions of the New Continent.* Trans. Helen Maria Williams. London: Longman, 1822.

——. *Relation historique aux régions équinoxiales du Noveau Continent, fait en 1799, 1800, 1801, 1802, 1803 et 1804, par Al. de Humboldt et A. Bondpland, ré-dige par Alexandre de Humboldt; avec un atlas géographique et physique.* 4 vols. Paris: F. Schoell, 1814–1825.

Humboldt, Alexander. *Researches Concerning the Institutions and Monuments of the Ancient Inhabitants of America, with Descriptions and Views of the Most Striking Scenes in the Cordilleras.* Trans. Helen Maria Williams. London: Longman, 1814.

———. *Vues des Cordillères, et monumens des peuples indigènes de l'Amérique.* Paris, 1810.

Huysmans, K. J. *Against Nature.* Trans. Robert Baldik. London: Penguin Classics, 1984.

Ingenieros, José. *Crónicas de viaje.* Ed. Aníbal Ponce. Vol. 5 of *Obras completas.* Buenos Aires: Ediciones L. J. Rosso, n.d.

———. *Dos páginas de psiquiatría criminal.* Buenos Aires: Librería Bredahl, 1900.

———. *La locura en la Argentina.* Ed. Aníbal Ponce. Vol. 12 of *Obras completas.* Buenos Aires: Ediciones L. J. Rosso, 1937.

———. *La psicopatología en el arte.* Buenos Aires: Editorial Losada, 1990.

———. *La simulación en la lucha por la vida.* Buenos Aires: Roggero-Ronal Editores, 1952.

———. "Valor de la psicopatología en la antropología criminal." *Archivos de Criminalogía Medicina Legal y Psiquiatría* 1 (1902): 1–11.

———. "Variedades: Nota sobre la psicología de los escritores." *Archivos de Psiquiatría, Criminología y Ciencias Afines* 7 (1908): 582–86.

Isaacs, Jorge. *María.* Ed. Gustavo Mejía. Caracas: Biblioteca Ayacucho, 1978.

Kearney, Michael. *The Winds of Ixtepeji: World View and Society in a Zapotec Town.* New York: Holt, Rinehart and Winston, 1972.

Kleinman, Arthur. *The Illness Narratives.* New York: Basic Books, 1988.

Kristeva, Julia. *Pouvoirs et limites de la psychanalyse: la révolte inime.* Paris: Fayard, 1996.

López Piñero, J. M. *Orígenes históricos del concepto de neurosis.* Madrid: Alianza Universidad, 1985.

Loyola, St. Ignatius. *The Spiritual Exercises.* Ed. Joseph Rickaby. London: Burns Oates and Washbourne, 1923.

Markus, Gyorgy. "Why Is There No Hermeneutics of Natural Sciences. Some Preliminary Theses." *Science in Context* 1, no. 1 (1987): 5–51.

Martin, Emily. *The Woman in the Body: A Cultural Analysis of Reproduction.* Boston: Beacon Press, 1987.

Mollien, Gaspard-Théodore. *Voyage dans la république de Colombia en 1823.* 2 vols. Paris: A. Bertrand, 1825.

Molloy, Sylvia. *At Face Value: Autobiographical Writing in Spanish America.* Cambridge: Cambridge University Press, 1991.

———. "Paraíso perdido y economía terrenal en *María.*" *Sin nombre* 14, no. 3 (1984): 36–55.

Moreau (de Tours), Jacques Joseph. *La psychologie morbide dans ses rapports avec la philosophie de l'histoire ou de l'influence des névropathies sur le dynamisme intellectuel.* Paris: Librairie Victor Masson, 1859.

Morel, Benedict. *Traité des dégénérescences physiques, intellectuelles et morales de l'espèce humaine,* 1857. Reprint, New York: Arno Press, 1976.

Museo de cuadros de costumbres. 4 vols. Bogotá: Biblioteca Banco Popular, 1973.

Nietzsche, Friedrich. *The Birth of Tragedy and the Genealogy of Morals.* Trans. Francis Golffing. New York: Doubleday and Company, 1956.

———. *Twilight of the Idols/The Anti-Christ.* Trans. R. J. Hollingdale. London: Penguin Books, 1990.

———. *On the Genealogy of Morals*. Trans. Walter Kaufmann and R. J. Hollingdale. Ed. Walter Kaufmann. New York: Vintage Books, 1969.

Nordau, Max. *Degeneration*. Lincoln: University of Nebraska Press, 1993.

Oliver, Kelly. *Family Values: Subjects between Nature and Culture*. New York: Routledge, 1997.

———. *Womanizing Nietzsche: Philosophy's Relation to the "Feminine."* New York: Routledge, 1995.

Pick, Daniel. *Faces of Degeneration: A European Disorder 1848–1918*. Cambridge: Cambridge University Press, 1989.

Picó, Fernando. *Al filo del poder*. Río Piedras: Editorial de la Universidad de Puerto Rico, 1993.

———. *Historia general de Puerto Rico*. Río Piedras: Ediciones Huracán, 1986.

Pombo, Manuel. *De Medellín a Bogotá*. Bogotá: Talleres de Tercer Mundo Editores, Instituto Colombiano de Cultura, Colcultura, 1992.

Pratt, Mary Louise. *Imperial Eyes: Travel Writing and Transculturation*. London: Routledge, 1992.

———. "Scratches on the Face of the Country; or, What Mr. Barrow Saw in the Land of the Bushmen." *Critical Inquiry* 12 (1985): 119–45.

Proust, Marcel. *Remembrance of Things Past*. Trans. C. K. Scott Moncrieff and Terence Kilmartin. New York: Vintage Books, 1982.

Quevedo Báez, M. "Cartilla higiénica." *Boletín de la Asociación Médica de Puerto Rico* 2, no. 18 (1904): 286–88.

Quintero Rivera, Angel G. *Patricios y plebeyos: burgueses, hacendados, artesanos y obreros*. Río Piedras: Ediciones Huracán, 1988.

Rama, Angel. *La ciudad letrada*. Hanover, N. H.: Ediciones del Norte, 1984.

Ramos, Julio. "A Citizen Body: Cholera in Havana (1833)." *Dispositio/N* 19, no. 46 (1996): 179–95.

———. *Desencuentros de la modernidad en América Latina: literatura y política en el siglo XIX*. Mexico: Fondo de Cultura Económica, 1989.

Ramos, Samuel. *Profile of Man and Culture in Mexico*. Trans. P. G. E. Austin: University of Texas Press, 1962.

Ramos Mejía, J.M. *La locura en la historia*. Buenos Aires: Félix Lajouane, 1895.

———. "Medicina legal: Informe sobre el estado mental del Sr. W." *Anales del departamento nacional de higiene* 19 (1897): 425–33.

———. *Las neurosis de los hombres célebres en la historia argentina*. Buenos Aires: La Cultura Argentina, 1915.

Riaño Jauma, Ricardo. *José Ingenieros y su obra literaria*. Havana: Arellano y Cía., 1933.

Romero, Laura. "Vanishing Americans: Gender, Empire and New Historicism." In *The Culture of Sentiment*, ed. Shirley Samuels. 115–27. New York: Oxford University Press, 1992.

Rose, Nikolas. *Inventing Our Selves: Psychology, Power and Personhood*. Cambridge: Cambridge University Press, 1996.

———. "Medicine, History and the Present." In *Reassessing Foucault: Power, Medicine and the Body*, eds. Colin Jones and Roy Porter, 48–72. London: Routledge, 1994.

Rosenberg, Charles E., and Janet Golden, eds. *Framing Disease: Studies in Cultural History.* N.J.: Rutgers University Press, 1992.

Samper, José M. *Ensayo sobre las revoluciones políticas y la condición social de las repúblicas colombianas (Hispanoamericanas) con un apéndice sobre la orografía y la población de la confederación granadina.* Vol. 52. Bogotá: Biblioteca popular de cultura colombiana, n.d.

Sarmiento, Domingo F. *Recuerdos de provincia.* Barcelona: Editorial Sopena, 1967.

Silva, José Asunción. *Obra completa.* Caracas: Biblioteca Ayacucho, 1977.

Soler, Ricaurte. *El positivismo argentino.* Panamá: Imprenta Nacional, 1959.

Sommer, Doris. *Foundational Fictions.* Berkeley: University of California Press, 1991.

Sontag, Susan. *Illness as Metaphor.* New York: Vintage, 1979.

Soto-Hall, M. *Revelaciones íntimas de Rubén Darío.* Buenos Aires: El Ateneo, 1925.

Stabb, Martin. *In Quest of Identity; Patterns in the Spanish American Essay of Ideas, 1890–1960.* Chapel Hill: University of North Carolina Press, 1967.

Stahl, A. "Difusión de la uncinaria y liga de defensa contra la anemia." *Boletín de la Asociación Médica de Puerto Rico* 3, no. 35 (1905): 155–64.

Stepan, Nancy Leys, and Sander L. Gilman. "Appropriating the Idioms of Science: The Rejection of Scientific Racism." *The Bounds at Roa: Perspectives on Hegemony and Resistance,* ed. Dominick Lapacra. 72–103. Ithaca: Cornell University Press, 1991:

Taine, Hippolite. *On Intelligence.* Trans. T. D. Haye. Vol. 2. New York: Henry Holt and Co., 1879.

Tapper, Melbourne. *In the Blood: Sickle Cell Anemia and the Politics of Race.* Philadelphia: University of Pennsylvania Press, 1998.

———. "Interrogating Bodies: Medico-Racial Knowledge, Politics, and the Study of a Disease." *Comparative Studies in Society and History* 37, no. 1 (1995): 76–93.

Taussig, Michael. *Shamanism, Colonialism and the Wild Man.* Chicago: Chicago University Press, 1987.

Vasconcelos, José. *La raza cósmica.* Buenos Aires: Espasa Calpe, 1948.

Velasco Madriñán, Luis C. *Jorge Isaacs, el caballero de las lágrimas.* Cali: Editorial América, 1942.

Vezzetti, Hugo. *La locura en la Argentina.* Buenos Aires: Editorial Paidós, 1985.

Zeno de Matos, Elena. *Manuel Zeno Gandía: documentos biográficos y críticos.* San Juan: 1955.

Zeno Gandía, Manuel. *La charca.* Ed. Enrique Laguerre. Caracas: Biblioteca Ayacucho, 1978.

———. *Higiene de la infancia al alcance de las madres de familia.* San Francisco: The History Company, 1891.

Index

University Press of New England publishes books under its own imprint and is the publisher for Brandeis University Press, Dartmouth College, Middlebury College Press, University of New Hampshire, Tufts University, and Wesleyan University Press.

About the author: Benigno Trigo is Assistant Professor in the Hispanic Languages and Literature Department at the State University of New York, Stony Brook campus.

Library of Congress Cataloging-in-Publication Data
Trigo, Benigno.
   Subjects of crisis : race and gender as disease in Latin America /
Benigno Trigo.
     p.   cm.
   Includes bibliographical references and index.
   ISBN 0–8195–6392–7 (cloth : alk. paper). — ISBN 0–8195–6393–5
(pbk. : alk. paper)
     1. Latin America—Civilization—Philosophy.   2. Sex role—Latin
America.   3. Diseases and literature—Latin America.   4. Latin
America—Race relations.   I. Title.   II. Title: Race and gender as
disease in Latin America.
F1408.3.T75   1999
305.8'0098—dc21   99–34295